Two I and a Thumb

by

Tim Montgomery

October 1996

Produced with help of
Second Chance

HEREFORDSHIRE
Lifestyles

Published by Tim Montgomery

Two Feet and a Thumb

First Published in 2001

by

Tim Montgomery
Brimfield
Ludlow
Shropshire

Copyright © Tim Montgomery 2001

ISBN 0 9540547 0 9

All rights reserved. No part of this publication may be reproduced, stored in a retrieval system, or transmitted in any form by any means, electronic, mechanical, photocopying, recording or otherwise, without the prior permission of the publishers.

Typeset and printed by
Record Printers Ltd
Bromyard, Herefordshire

FOREWORD

"Two Feet and a Thumb" is Tim Montgomery's autobiography. Tim suffered a severe head injury at the age of seven which affected his life thereafter. He was in a coma for three months following the accident and ended up requiring special schooling.

Some considerable time after completing his formal education Tim decided to join the "Second Chance" scheme at Ludlow College to improve his reading and writing skills. The "Second Chance" scheme is a basic skills literacy or numeracy course ~or~adults with learning difficulties or those who may,some way have missed out on earlier educational opportunities . This autobiography is a demonstration of Tim's achievement.

Tim's aim in life was to become a farmer. As can be seen from his story he has gone a long way towards achieving this ambition despite the problems created by his accident.

"Two Feet and a Thumb" is all Tim's own work. The only contribution from "Second Chance" staff has been in providing typing and word processing facilities and assistance and some editorial suggestions on presentation and clarification of some episodes.

Tim's recollection of incidents and detail is astonishing and despite the various setbacks and difficulties he encountered his story is not lacking humour.

The title is derived from Tim's preferred means of transport!

FH

RJT

DM

"Second Chance" Ludlow

April 1998

TIMOTHY BATTLES ON...

© Worcester Evening News

TIMOTHY MONTGOMERY, aged 20, has the same name as a famous soldier, and, like Field Marshall Montgomery, he has fought a battle and won.

A patient at the Orthopaedic Hospital, Timothy has just had an operation on his knee to rectify damage caused when he slipped from a ramp while pushing a loaded wheelbarrow.

In itself the fact that he was pushing a wheelbarrow and doing heavy work was nothing less than a miracle. Timothy was seriously injured as a small boy, and became very much like a spastic—unable to walk, to talk, to co-ordinate his muscles. But perseverance and strength of character won the battle against misfortune and Timothy regained his strength sufficiently to carry on with his schooling and later to help his father on their smallholding.

Timothy was seven, and on his way to post a Christmas card when he fell from his bicycle and damaged his head.

He lay unconscious for three months. When he left hospital, one year and two months later, he had to learn to walk and talk all over again.

Timothy is the son of Mr and Mrs J. G. Montgomery, The Mount, Rochford, Tenbury Wells.

Incidents recalled in my life

I was born on 20th September 1950 which was a Thursday. My father had been a National Hunt jockey, and he used to tell a story that after a serious accident when racing his obituary had inadvertently been put in the local newspaper, however he was very much alive and met my mother when she was a stablegirl working at stables in West Kirby.

My parents married in February 1947, the year of the freezing winter. My elder brother Rupert was born in April 1948, so that made him two and a half when I arrived. Home at that time being a riding school in West Kirby which my parents ran.

My family moved up to Appleby in Westmorland, in 1951, where my parents bought a smallholding on which at the time there was a herd of Ayrshire cows which were replaced over a period of time by a herd of jersey cattle. I vividly recall the building of the silage pit, and whilst playing around the pit with my brother with our water pistols losing the top of mine in the pit. How very upset I was, however to my joy in the winter, when silage was being extracted for the cattle what emerged at the top, my water pistol, imagine my excitement. That silage pit caused a number of incidents, cousin Sue leant on one of the walls under construction and it collapsed, fortunately not injuring anyone.

During the time in Appleby we children had a very happy time There were good banks on the farm which made for excellent sledging and we were usually joined on these occasions by Sheila and Kathleen the girls from the farm next door.

When Elizabeth was born on the 11th October 1955, Rupert and I decided to take her to market as she was no good for playing with and we needed lots of help to build the bonfire. I liked the tractors father had and remember us having over a period a grey Fergusson tractor, a Fordson and a David Brown.

I was rushed into hospital at two and a half years with appendicitis for an emergency operation, and then I had to go to the hospital in Carlisle again when I was five, by train with my father, for a tonsil operation, but good old dad bought me a toy tractor to play with while I was in the hospital.

I started school in September 1955 at Ormside, Appleby. This was a small village school with under 20 children The head teacher was Miss Forbes, and she was also the only teacher, all we children sat in the same classroom. During this time I was Little Jack Horner in the school Pantomime and I especially enjoyed the school trips to Blackpool and Morcambe. My dad took us down to school, seven children in all from neighbouring farms, all crammed in the van along with a small milk churn which he delivered daily to the Cottage Hospital. During one winter when the lane was blocked we had an exciting trip for we children, going across the fields part way to avoid the snow blocked lane.

In Spring of 1957 we were about to move to Thirlthorpe in Yorkshire, however before moving I learnt to ride the two wheeler bicycle, before my elder brother Rupert.

Unfortunately, although we sold the smallholding in Appleby, the property at Thirlthorpe fell through, so we moved to West Kirby, Cheshire and stayed with our maternal grandmother (big Gran's) for about six months. During this period I had a term in the primary school in West Kirby, quite a shock after a small village school. The first boy that I sat by kept pinching me, so I was moved by the teacher.

In the December just before Christmas, we moved to Rattlinghope, Shropshire. Our new home was a three bedroomed cottage with a reasonably large garden. My brother and I shared a bedroom. The cottage was situated in a hollow in the countryside. We started to explore our new surroundings.

However on the 3rd January I was going down the hill to post the last of my Christmas thank you letters on my bicycle when I skidded and bumped my head as I fell off and hit the ground. After that I can't recall anything until I came round in the neurology wing, of Smethwick Hospital, Birmingham after being unconscious for three months.

Apparently I was found by Mr.Butler and his friend. Mr.Butler had a small dairy farm just down the road from our cottage. He picked me up and took me home. My mother didnt have a vehicle, as my Father was away in West Kirby so Mr.Butler then took mother and I to the Doctors surgery in Bishops Castle.

After a brief examination Dr Penny took us to the Royal Shrewsbury Hospital, and then to Lopthorne Hospital were I was X-rayed, before being transferred to Smethick Neurology Department by ambulance.

My mother spent the first two weeks at my bedside, but as my unconsciousness continued my mother had to return to the needs of the family. Visiting with my father as much as possible. I also caught Chicken Pox while still unconscious, which added to my problems. I can vaguely recall feeling at times as if I was driving, driving but I could never stop. Sister Doughty used to come to my bedside regularly and pinch me to see if there was any reaction.

As I regained consciousness my toy Noddy was there to keep me company, as I lay in my bed unable to walk or talk. My special Nurse was called Doreen Capewell, who had a son just six months older than I, we keep in touch to this day.

I was taken home by ambulance for a week in April for the occasion of my brothers tenth birthday. The ambulance men couldn't find our cottage, and unable to speak at all just nod or shake my head I couldn't help with directions but oh joy on a sharp bend not far from the cottage I remembered there was an old tractor dumped in the side, yes there it was, we were on the right road. Almost there, Dad was standing outside the village Pub, owned by Mr. & Mrs Champion, which he was painting.

How pleased I was to be home. However the week went past all too quickly and it was back to Smethwick Hospital, and to my continuing battle to learn to walk and talk again. We had a black and white T.V. in the hospital, and my favourite programme was the "Lone Ranger".

In June 1958 I left the hospital and came home again still unable to walk and talk, other than nod or shake my head, but I could understand what people said. Elizabeth was my companion and at two and a half she would bring toys for me. But alas, no television at home, in fact no electricity, when it got dark Mum or Dad lit the paraffin lamps.

Three times a week I was taken for Physiotherapy, the chief Physiotherapist was Miss Bloor. I was collected by ambulance and Mum or Dad always came with me. I also went to ENT one day a week on Fridays and Mr. Paulett was my Speech Therapist, and the latter used to play football in his spare time for Shrewsbury Town Football Club. I remember him getting me to say, "My Pa's car is a Jaguar" amongst, of course, lots of other speech exercises. I found it very hard work learning to talk again. My first clear words were one day when we were waiting for an ambulance to come and take home my Dad and myself, I said, "I wish they would come", my Dad was over joyed. Slowly, but surely my speech improved.

Aunty Brenda came and brought me a blue budgie which I called "Pretty Patty", Rupert also was not forgotten he received a tortoise. The idea in giving me the budgie was that in trying to get the budgie to speak I would be helping my own speech, unfortunately, after only a few months, the budgie cage was accidently knocked over and the budgie escaped. However one of the ambulance men who took me to Physiotherapy bred budgies, and after a short time he kindly gave me another budgie, to try to replace the one I had lost.

I had a calipur fitted to my right leg and this assisted my walking and in March 1959 I started school in Rattlinghope, going for just half a day a week. Once again it was a very small village school with only eleven children all in the same class. My brother Rupert was with me and the teacher was called Miss Horrocks, however, I was only there for about a month, before it was Easter, and our family moved to Lydbury North, in Shropshire.

My Dad had a job as a Herdsman to a Herd of Jersey cattle, at Plowden Hall, and we moved into quite a big house. Our neighbours were Mr. & Mrs. Evans, and Mr. Evans was a farm worker for Mr. J. Naughton, a neighbouring farmer. It was a very nice rural area to live in and we children set out to explore the area. On a couple of occasions I walked on my own to see my Dad at work, a considerable undertaking as it was two miles away. My mother was worried at my absence and with no telephone, unable to try and check on my whereabouts.

I started at yet another new school, this time Lydbury North Primary School. This school was a little larger than my past school having between 50 and 60 pupils. I had one term in the infants, and then moved into the Juniors with Mrs. Beman for two years. I well recall it was half a mile to school each way.

In September it was my ninth birthday and I had a small party, and then three weeks later, on Elizabeth's fourth birthday, I broke my wrist playing football. Off to Shrewsbury hospital again, calling at the doctors in Bishops Castle first just to make sure it was broken. The wrist was put in plaster, and three weeks off school was ordered. Hooray!

In the garden it was decided to pull up a privet hedge, to make room for the growing of vegetables, and we children were pressed into action collecting up the stones. The incentive was that we were being paid for our respective pile of stones.

December came and it had been arranged for me to go into the Royal Shrewsbury Hospital, on Thursday 10th, I remember listening to "Brain of Britain" on the long wave of the radio whilst in my hospital bed prior to another operation. I was going to have a leg muscle altered which was affecting my toe and causing me to trip. The operation was performed by Mr. Rose and I had eleven stitches. The operation was a success, and after the plaster was removed nine days later, I started physiotherapy, and gradually I found it easier to walk.

Unfortunately I was not fit enough to attend the school Christmas Party that year, but I was not forgotten as three school friends made a special visit to my house to bring me a present from the party.

Returning to school in January 1960 after the muscle operation to my leg. I found that the infant and junior playground had been combined, this had necessitated the removal of a wall, and the whole area being resurfaced.

In February, Doreen Caple and her son Robert came to stay for a week, the former had been my special nurse in Smethick after my accident and she was pleased to see my progress. The latter was also monitored by Mr. Campbell Connelly, the surgeon who had operated on me at Smethick, moved to St. Bartholemews, London, and between 1960 and 1963 I went up to London once a year to see my surgeon.

During the early part of 1960, due to a lot of heavy rainfall periods, there was a great deal of flooding in the area of Shropshire. In Shrewsbury at my old Physiotherapy unit there was a landslip, and the unit had to be closed. From our house you could see flooded land all around, even the lane to school was passable only in wellingtons. Walcot Hall lakes were flooded as far as the eye could see.

Father changed his job to become an Ambulance driver in London, coming home as his shift pattern would allow. He was eventually transferred to Shrewsbury in 1961. Mother, meanwhile, looked after horses with Mrs Plowden, going to work on a motor bike.

On July 26th, Heather Claire my youngest sister was born, sadly she was one of twin, and the other twin was stillborn. This meant that mother, Big Gran, cousin Sue and all we children, had been born on the same day of the week.

In September I went into the top class in my Primary school, Mr. Moss was my teacher, and my brother by this time was at the High school in Bishops Castle.

On Christmas Eve that year, my brother Rupert, friend John and myself set out to go for a walk and pick some holly. The weather had been freezing and the ground was frozen. Whilst John was up the tree picking holly, Rupert was trying to break the ice on a pond, so that the labrador dog that was with us would fall in. However the reverse happened and it was Rupert who fell in, and we other two laughed so much that John nearly fell out of the holly tree.

During my last year at the primary school, discussions were taking place as to where I should go for my senior schooling. It was thought that I would benefit from special schooling which would cater for my needs, this meant looking for a school with boarding facilities as there were none close to my home. An interview was arranged at a school in Nottingham but children here were very handicapped, and it was not considered suitable. Then I went to Exhall Grange School, Coventry for an interview, but unfortunately no places were available, so for one term only I attended White Nurse Manor, Broadstairs, Kent. Transferring to Exhall Grange as a place become available, and as a result this school was to become my home in term time for nearly five years.

Exhall Grange school was a mixed school with about 300 pupils, the ratio of pupils was about 200 boys to 100 girls. All pupils were residential and the age range was between 5 and 17 years. About 40 - 50 pupils were handicapped and the remainder partially sighted.

The school had 4 new Halls of residence called Warwick, Windsor, Avon and Kenilworth, the latter housed the girls, plus two old army huts called Canterbury and Lancaster, and I was placed in the latter. Inside Lancaster there was a long central corridor, from which bedrooms led off on both sides, these bedrooms mainly contained two bunk beds. additionally there were two bathrooms and a common room.

January 3rd 1963 was my first day at Exhall Grange, and the headmaster was Mr.Harshall. We were expected to get up at 7-30am, when one of the house matrons would come round. My house matron was Miss Stanley. After washing dressing and making beds, we were expected to march down to the dining hall, along with pupils from Canterbury for breakfast at 8-20am Sometimes the march down to breakfast was not a pleasant experience due to the weather or time of the year. Breakfast usually consisted of sloppy porridge from Monday to Friday, with bread and marmalade and a cup of tea. On Saturday and Sunday we had cornflakes, and the special Sunday breakfast treat was either under or overcooked boiled eggs.

Lessons commenced at 9-00 am after an assembly to which the whole school came with the exception of the Roman Catholic pupils. We had a morning break at 10.30, and lunch was at 12-30pm, after which we could return to our rooms and check for any post etc. Afternoon school started at 1-45pm until 4pm. We were then free for 30 minutes until 4-30pm when we had tea. Older pupils returned to the classrooms for prep from 5pm to 6pm. If the weather was fine pupils were allowed free time earlier, and could go out into the grounds under supervision, this was usually only possible in the summer months, depending on age and the member of staff on duty bedtimes were flexible.

A couple of weeks after starting at Exhall Grange I had to go into the sick bay with a temperature and during this time the weather deteriorated rapidly. We had a tremendous frost about -32, and this resulted in fantastic icicles. The snow that year lasted for about ten weeks, the biggest freeze since 1947. All the pipes in our huts froze, so water for washing became a problem.

Gradually I got to know the staff, I recall Mr Reed who taught English, Mr Steeper P.E. and Games, Miss Hardesty - partially sighted pupils, Mr Rice and Miss Lewis whom we referred to as the "Welsh Dragon" behind her back.

New school buildings were being erected to replace in the main the old army huts which had previously housed a large portion of the school. A smashing room was provided initially as a weaving room, on the first floor, this was later converted to a photography room and the teacher in charge was Miss Somerville.

A subject that I really enjoyed was pottery and over the years I made a lamp base, vase and various other pieces of pottery. Another of my favourite subjects was Maths, I certainly was very adept at working out how many seconds had to pass before the term ended.

My first summer at Exhall Grange we had a school trip to Rhyl by train, spending the day on the beach and going round the fairground.

My father went on a years course during 1964 - 65, the course was on "Caring for the handicapped," and then he worked in homes for the handicapped in the south of England. He was hoping to move the family including grandma and grandpa to the south, and the house in Lydbury North was put up for sale, when it proved to be taking a long time to sell the idea gradually fizzled out and the family stayed put.

The 12th July 1967 was my last day at Exhall Grange, I was sixteen years old. I returned home to Lydbury North, Rupert was also leaving his school days behind, and planning to go to Lancaster University in the autumn.

It was decided that as we had about 2 1/2 acres at home, and with the addition of some rented land it would provide an opportunity for me to start a small Jersey Herd, and my mother would act as my advisor.

During the summer of 1967 Rupert and I started taking down an old outhouse at home, with Dads help when he was also at home. The outhouse had deteriorated badly and one of the main beams had rotted through making the building unsafe.

One day whilst busy working on the outhouse, the telephone rang, and Dad went to answer it, leaving me with a fully loaded wheelbarrow balanced on a plank, telling me to wait until his return before moving the barrow. However I felt I could manage, unfortunately the barrow tipped and whilst trying to control it I damaged my knee struggling to keep the barrow upright. This resulted in a hospital visit, where my knee was bandaged and I was told to rest for a fortnight in bed. Fortunately the pirate Radio stations which had been closed down, continued with Radio Caroline broadcasting from Off-shore stations, one in the north and one in the south, these were a godsend during my enforced rest.

One day a Mr Walker turned up and wanted to buy our home in Lydbury North, this was a surprise as we had virtually given up the idea of moving. However this didn't happen immediately and in fact it was the 5th February in the following year 1968 before we finally moved from our home.

Meanwhile Mum was busy that summer helping Mr Philip Gough to groom and clip his horses ready for showing. Mum had been introduced to the latter by Lady Plowden, via the pony club and as Mr Gough did not have any children, my sisters Elizabeth and Heather were asked to ride and show the ponies at various events during the summer. They were quite successful collecting a number of prizes.

Rupert, when not helping with the building demolition, was busy in the garden and kept us in vegetables that summer, as he had many previous years. In fact he often won prizes at local shows for his vegetables and flowers, in particular sweet peas.

My knee injury meant I had to go back to Shrewsbury Royal Infirmary, (the old one) which I well remembered from my past injuries and renew my acquaintance with Miss Bloor for physiotherapy for about 2/3 weeks.

On the 11th October which also happened to be Elizabeth's twelfth birthday, Rupert left to begin his first term at Lancaster University. Mum and I accompanied him and his luggage in the Fiat 600. Rupert went into digs in Morecambe for his first year as the University Halls of Residence which were still being completed.

At this time, now knowing that the house was definitely being sold, Dad and Mum began a house search in the south of England, Dad still working at a home for the handicapped, Chaleigh Heritage in Sussex.

However, after discussing the moving house situation, mother revealed that she didn't really want to move to the south of England, as she felt that my sisters were settled in the Shropshire area with regard to friends, schools, Pony club etc. Rupert was at university in the north of England, and so it was decided that dad would look for another job closer to Shropshire. He was fortunate in finding a job quite soon with the Spastic Society at Kyre Park near Tenbury Wells.

It was during this period that an outbreak of 'Foot and Mouth' occurred in our area. A farmer had taken two infected cattle to Oswestry market and the out break spread from this incident being particularly bad in Shropshire, Denbighshire and Cheshire.

At the beginning of January we got snowed in for 4/5 days. We dug and drove, and dug and drove, until we got the quarter mile to the main lane. Great achievement!!! A day later the weather turned milder and all the snow melted!!! Elizabeth my elder sister got a place at Wakeman School, Shrewsbury, and it was decided that mother would share the school run with Mr. Moss, our headmaster at Lydbury, alternate weeks as his daughter was also going to Wakeman, and the girls needed transport the 8 miles to the railway station at Craven Arms.

We finally found a small holding at Munderfield, near Bromyard, which was called Claypits and consisted of about 5 and a half acres and we moved in on 5th February 1968. Dad had an oil fired Esse put in, in the kitchen, and an oil fire in the sitting room especially to keep Granny warm, who now lived with us. Elizabeth moved to a school in Bromyard and Heather attended the local infant school.

Dad started knocking down unsuitable outhouses, pigeries etc. and building up cow stalls and calf pens, ready to start a small Jersey Herd for me to run on a day to day basis with help from my mother.

In April Philip Gough invited us over, i.e. Dad, Mum, and myself, and we purchased after viewing, 2 jersey cows that had been twins. actually only paying for one, as the other cow called Rosie was in poor condition. Gradually we brought Rosie back into condition, however Ruby the other cow was dry at the time of purchase. Meanwhile we carried on with the building work and muggins had to do all the concrete mixing !!!! Mr. Hancock came over one evening, the man who used to own our house, and said that he had a concrete mixer that we could borrow. Whoopee!!!, no more mixing by hand.

Then we went over to Coventry to collect a milking bale dad had bought. We got it back safely, and then we had to produce more concrete to stand it on.

On 11th July a very wet and stormy night Ruby had her

Jersey/Charolais bull calf. Unfortunately Ruby had milk fever and we had to get out Mr Stokes the vet. The calf was called Charlie, named really by Joe Griffiths, who when he first saw the calf said, "Oh! he's a good Charlie." Joe also took the surplus milk away to feed to his pigs, which did so very well and had such wonderful coats, as a result of all that extra milk.

I did some of the milking but Mum was really the expert at hand milking, and she could fill a pail in no time at all, the cows were always quiet to milk. Ruby however fed her own calf and as a result Charlie grew rapidly. At this time we were also building a six cubicle addition to the milking bale, so that we would be able to cope with more cows in the future.

At the time of purchase "Claypits" was not on mains water. although it was promised as a firm prospect which was then cancelled. Mother, and the family were so mad that the former wrote to the Prime Minister, "Uncle Harold Wilson" protesting strongly at the decision. To cut a long story short we finally had mains water, just three months before it was decided we should move again in 1969, however I will come to that shortly. Dad meanwhile used to bring home daily 2 or 3 jerry cans full of mains water, just to keep us in fresh drinking water.

We had so much grass that year that Joe Griffiths said he would cut it for hay, and he would take it all less fifty bales which we could set aside for our own use. In the summer as part of the Spastic Society Fete at Kyre Park, Dad suggested they had a small Gymkhana, and my sisters went to the Gymkhana to show off Philip Gough's ponies.

We sold Charlie to Joe Griffiths, and purchased twin heifer calves, to rear and use up the surplus milk. These calves had been born on Mrs Thomas' our next door neighbours farm on which Joe acted as manager to the dairy Herd and in addition ran the Hop enterprise. The farm was called "Queuesop Farm". In fact the field next to our boundary was the one on which the hops were grown.

It was fascinating to watch the hop picking at such close quarters, from the strings being set up in the Spring until the harvesting in September, when the hops were sprayed at ground level to kill off the leaves, then the strings were cut, and they would be taken on a loaded trailer to the Harvester in the farm yard which would separate the Hops from the leaves and strings. The hops going into the kiln for drying.

We had at this time two Siamese cats called Bimbo and Candy, I well recall Bimbo one day just after he had been fed going out, five minutes later he was back with a large rabbit in his mouth. Mum naturally booted him out, only for me to find a little later one large dead rabbit deposited in my wellington boot.

In the autumn I started digging out some quite large and some small apple and pear trees, some of the smaller trees needed very little digging and if I left them overnight after digging round the root, they had usually been toppled by the wind overnight. Joe sawed up the wood to use on his fire, the timber being no good to our family as we were oil fired. We also had quite a lot of damson trees, which Rupert picked and any surplus fruit we took to Tenbury Wells market along with any surplus butter which we occasionally had.

I kept having trouble with my right Knee slipping out so an appointment was made for me to see Mr Slee at Hereford General Hospital on 31st. October 1968 and he was amazed that I could even walk on the leg as I had a very bad "slipping Patella".

During the autumn we had a contractor in to fell a few more trees, and on Christmas Eve it started to snow, so that Year we had a "WHITE CHRISTMAS". It wasn't until Boxing Day that I was admitted to Hospital ready to have my knee operation the next day.

I was admitted to the Harriet Davies Ward in Hereford General Hospital, and spent three and a half weeks in the hospital recovering from the operation. The knee kept leaking, which made for slow progress, and I had 17 stitches removed finally. A nurse who I have kept in touch with since that time was Jill Taylor (now Keddle).

After leaving the hospital I returned home on crutches. I returned home, to a very mild January. I still had my leg in plaster, this was removed mid February when the weather had turned colder and much more seasonal, ie. heavy frosts. Mum meanwhile took over all the milking, I tried to help with the butter making but some days it just wouldn't take.

After the plaster was removed from my leg I had to go to Bromyard Hospital for Physiotherapy - this hospital was about a mile outside Bromyard on the Worcester road, now unfortunately closed.

Spring came and the cows went out to grass. Rosie calved, a Charolais cross bull calf, however the calf unfortunately was not very strong and we had quite a few visits from the vet. Joe got me a couple more heifer calves again to use up the surplus milk, as he had done the previous year, taking the original calves back at about twelve weeks.

My parents felt that "Claypits" was not altogether suitable for the family, so decided to put it on the property market for sale. We had done quite a few improvements and alterations and also it was now on mains water which should make it a much more attractive proposition to any would be purchaser.

A young couple from Warwickshire area wanted to purchase, so we set about looking for a new home.

Sadly in June of that year Gran fell and fractured her pelvis and she only lived for a further fourteen days, dying the day after Prince Charles was Invested as the Prince of Wales at Caernarvon Castle.

Initially mum and dad were interested in properties as far away as Somerset and Devon, and I recall them going to visit some in

Auntie Brenda's Morris 1100. However, a few were sold before we were in a position to negotiate, and anyway my parents finally decided to concentrate their search in the Bromyard, Tenbury Wells area.

They visited the 'Mount' Rochford near Tenbury Wells which had been empty for approximately eighteen months, and liked the property, but realised that it needed quite a bit of work doing on it, as it had no bathroom, only a closet down the garden, and the ceiling in the kitchen was falling down etc. Anyway a decision was made to go ahead and purchase as the house was quite large, had a conservatory, a good garden, and outbuildings, and in addition we were able to purchase approximately five acres.

Before moving in Dad and I put new floor timbers, and sheets of hardboard to form a ceiling above the kitchen. However we decided to make 8th September moving day, as it was important to get the girls into their new schools at the start of the autumn term. Elizabeth went to Kidderminster High School, and Heather to the junior school in Tenbury Wells.

It was not long before Handleys the builders moved in to do the major jobs. We had a bathroom put in next to the kitchen, a new concrete floor put in the kitchen, and a new aga cooker.

Dad continued to work at Kyre Park and also supervised alterations to the outbuildings.

Joe had the heifer calves back and as we sold Ruby and the calf before we moved, only Rosie came to the "Mount" We were getting about three and a half buckets of milk a day, and making butter with any surplus.

September 20th was my nineteenth birthday, and I decided to take the day off and spend the day in Worcester, catching the bus from Tenbury Wells.

Arthur O'Toole whose wife had worked with Dad at Kyre Park came and helped us at the weekends, in our adaptation of one of the outbuildings into a calf rearing unit. We needed to plaster all the walls in order to prevent the calves licking any lime out of the original walls. Guess who did all the mixing of the plaster? Yes muggins again.

The building was ready, the calf pens had been constructed and the first calves arrived on the 31st. October 1969 at about 5.40pm, on quite a cold and frosty evening. The calves were Fresian / Hereford and as they were the first six calves in our new unit, they were each given an initial letter as their name ie. A, F. We reared them on BOCM calf milk and Quicklets, during the same period as rearing these calves we continued to lay more concrete and get things generally ship shape.

The builders were still with us, Mr Horace Handley the builder put in a septic tank, and again we had an oil fire put in the dining room which was so efficient, it heated the whole house. We also blanked off the attic rooms, and put polythene across the floor of the attics to prevent heat loss and any leaks from the roof penetrating into the main house. A fortnight before Christmas the kitchen was sufficiently ready for the Aga to be lit. What Bliss!!!

We carried on with the concreting putting a new floor in the stable, in order to enable us to put the original batch of calves in their loose, before we sold them on.

The next batch of calves came in on a Friday, yes, it was the 13th and the month was February. A great deal of snow had fallen and it was very cold. Unfortunately we lost one of this batch. She was named "O" and known as little Olly, and unfortunately it was she who kicked the bucket when she was only ten days old. We obviously had occasional problems like any rearer, but we were learning all the time and getting more experienced in rearing calves. Our local vet at that time was Mr. Cracknell. Mum whilst assisting me with the calves was also engaged in breaking in ponies, some coming from Philip Gough.

The second batch of calves minus one were weaned, put loose in the stable, before being sold to the same purchaser as the original batch. We left purchasing any more calves through the summer as calf prices were high, and we were giving thought to what improvements we could make for future calf rearing enterprises.

We went down to Devon to get ideas from a calf rearing unit, and eventually decided to put down a new concrete base 6" deep and 21' by 32' , leaving the calf pens as they were for the time being, and putting up three concrete loose box sections on the concrete base, this giving us the flexibility to use them for horses or calves, as required.

This period was during the time of the Dutch Elm disease which tragically swept the country, and we had to have contractors in to fell three trees which were affected. The first tree felled was rotten all the way through, the next tree was partially rotted, and the final tree was in good condition.

We spent a great deal of our time fencing, in order to keep our stock in, and prevent our neighbours sheep from encroaching on our land.

July 1970, found us mowing the 4 acre field. Dad didn't think it was suitable for making hay, but I started turning, the mown grass with a hay rake. After about a week of turning in which we had had only a little rain, John Gough, the elder brother of Philip Gough, brought over his baler, and I estimated that we would get about 120 bales and Surprise, Surprise we got exactly 120 bales.

Rupert continued to be Head Gardener, when he was on vacation from University and in fact completed his course in June of that year.

Dad had resigned from Kyre Park, so as he was unemployed he had more time to devote to the building works around the house etc. In August, one Saturday evening, the day before friends from Yorkshire (Jim, Doreen, and Michael) were due to visit. Dad developed a severe pain in his stomach. Doctor Burnett called and said that Dad was to go to Hospital immediately, as it was very serious. Dad was successfully operated on that same night by a surgeon called Mr. Thomas.

Rupert took a temporary job at a television showroom in Kidderminster, and then went to work for Currys in Hereford shortly afterwards.

Dad came out of hospital towards the end of August, still with a long way to go before he was fully recovered. We still had to put the roof on over the three newly constructed loose boxes and he was frustrated that he was not fit enough to help.

Car maintenance was also on the agenda, and when Dad felt better, he had yet another go at putting a better engine in our Triumph Herald, with the assistance of a block and tackle. Rupert and Dad reckoned they could change the engine in 45 minutes.

In September I went to see Mr. Slee, the surgeon, who had operated on my knee in the past, as the knee was still slipping, and in his opinion, I required a further operation, so I was put on the waiting list.

However Dad was readmitted for a further operation in December 1970, and I remember that Rupert brought home a colour television on loan for the family to watch over the Christmas period.

The flooring of the calf house had already been completed, and Dad managed to obtain an old prefabricated bungalow, which was brought up by two men from Southampton, who erected the prefab onto the existing base. Starting about 7-30a.m. and completing the erection by about 11.00p.m.

January 1971, saw the the arrival of a great deal of rain, and the bungalow and cottage just down the hill from the Mount were flooded.

February 9th 1971, I reached my turn on the hospital waiting list and was admitted to the Agnes Hunt Orthopeadic Hospital in Gobowen, in readiness for a further operation on my knee. In this hospital they were fortunate enough to have a film theatre and on my first evening I watched the film "The King and I", which I enjoyed very much. My operation was scheduled for the following Saturday, and from the Tuesday of my admission whilst undergoing tests I also had plenty of free time to socialise and also use the hospital swimming pool. I was particularly pleased to find that there were a number of other young people with which to pass the time.

Mr. Slee, the same surgeon who had operated on me in Hereford General hospital, performed my second knee operation, the operation lasted just over an hour and I had 21 stitches which were removed after 10 days, but my leg was in plaster for a total of 4 weeks and 5 days.

During the time my leg was in plaster I went to occupational therapy classes. In charge was a Mrs. Gwyneth Davies, and it transpired that her maiden name was Janis and she had been a fellow pupil at Bishops Castle High School with my brother Rupert. In addition there were 5 student occupational therapists. They were called Wendy, from Northumberland, Nicky from South Africa, Jane from Leicestershire, Hilary from Manchester and Sarah but I forget were she hailed from. They all promised to come to my 21st birthday later in the year, but none of them arrived.!!!!

After Mr Slee had checked my leg and the plaster was removed, I was allowed to go home, Father picking me up at about 5p.m. It was good to be home, but I missed all my new friends in the hospital I had to attend physiotherapy twice a week for a further couple of weeks in Tenbury Wells hospital. However, it had all been worthwhile as the operation was a success and I know found walking considerably easier, and my knee was no longer slipping.

In April I was fit enough to start going with Robert Handley in his car to John Gough's Farm daily. Robert was an agricultural student, and I did odd jobs around the farm, including stacking hay bales and bringing the cows in from the field ready for milking, eventually I received £10 for my efforts and I put the money towards the purchase of a calf of my own, a Fresian/Charolais Bull calf.

I purchased the calf at Tenbury market, bidding for him on my own. When the calf was delivered home, only Mum and Heather were there to be surprised, as Dad was once again away working in the South of England at a home for the handicapped.

The calf which I decided to call Sampson was duly installed in the calf house and he was about 10 days old. Shortly afterwards it was Heathers tenth birthday and she decided to have her birthday games, in the unoccupied part of the calf house much to the surprise of Sampson.

The calf continued to grow well, and on the first Saturday in August the whole family went to Tenbury Show, at this time it was still held on Palmers Meadow, where the Tenbury swimming pool has since been built.

At the end of August John Gough was ready to harvest the oats, and it was arranged that David Nosworthy, the new farm worker, would do the baling and muggins would do the bale stacking.

On the Saturday evening preceding my twenty first birthday, I was given a lift down to the Tally Ho Pub in Broad Heath, and had a smashing evening in the company of Robert Handley, David Nosworthy, and others in the pub that evening. On the actual day I was twenty one, the 20th September, I had a birthday cake and family presents etc. Rupert unfortunately couldn't be with us as he was now working for Littlewoods in Sunderland.

Sampson continued to grow, and I weaned him and put him in a pen. Rosie calved during the month and I purchased another calf to go with Rosie's calf, both calves were heifers. I fed them initially on Rosie's milk diluted to 2/3 milk to 1/3 water, Jersey milk being so very rich. I continued going daily to John Gough's Farm still doing odd jobs as required.

Mum took more horses on a livery basis, using the stables now completed. This meant she was kept very busy riding out, schooling and mucking out. I helped when I came home from Hill Top Farm, mucking out Rosie's box and also the horses boxes.

January 1972, we noticed an advert for calf rearers in the "Hereford Times," we contacted the advertiser, who came to see our calf rearing set up. He agreed to send us calves, however we waited and waited, and finally he telephoned us saying that he was able to get his calves reared cheaper elsewhere.

Therefore on 16th February I hitched a lift to Kidderminster, put in a couple of bids for a charolais calf, to no avail, and then I hitched a lift home again. The next day Wednesday, was Mum and Dad's Silver wedding anniversary. Mum gave me a lift up to High House cross roads, and from their I got a lift with a farmer all the way to Hereford Market. I waited for the charolais calves to come in, before I made any bids, having already been round the pens and inspected the calves. A charolais calf was knocked down to me for £41. Having sold Sampson, and the heifer calves when they were weaned, I was now ready to use my cash towards more stock. I sought out John Yarnold in the market and he agreed to take the calf and myself home, fortunately he hadn't made any purchases so there was plenty of room in his van. I named the new calf Silver as it was my parents anniversary.

Shortly afterwards I went down to Tenbury Market and met Mr & Mrs George there, (I had previously met Mrs George as she was the district nurse who had checked my knee after my discharge from hospital). During our conversation, I mentioned that I was looking for some calves to rear on a contract basis, and as a result agreed to rear some calves for Mr George in the near future.

In the middle of April, 4 calves arrived for me to rear on behalf of Mr. George, and this was the start of my days as a "Contract calf rearer "I successfully reared these calves, so once again I hitched to Hereford and put an advert in the "Hereford Times" saying Contract Calf Rearer available, apply Newnham Bridge 391.

I received one reply from a Mr Bishop at Stoke Prior. He came out with his brother to see our calf rearing set up, obviously liked what he saw and agreed to send calves for rearing. Just by chance we had a ginger kitten looking for a good home, which they decided they would like to have. A few weeks later after the vet had given the kitten an M.O.T their comment was "That's a pedigree Welsh cat" for a common moggie so they must have been pleased.

The first calves from the Bishops arrived on the Saturday prior to the end of May, a Bank Holiday weekend. There were a dozen calves, a mixed bunch of breeds and not very strong looking calves either. They were about a week old and the vets comments when he first saw them indicated their state, as he said, "They obviously don't rear them, they ranch them". However, we managed to rear all to weaning bar one which unfortunately kicked the bucket. These calves were moved to a large pen together and when they were about six weeks old the Bishops rang up on a day when my parents had gone for a few days holiday to Angelsey, saying they were bringing over more calves, which they had just purchased.

Without any assistance I cleaned out as many individual pens as I could manage in the time available, and the new calves arrived and were duly installed.

We kept the original calves until they were twelve weeks old, when the Bishops collected them, and the second batch considering their hasty introduction continued to do quite well with only the occasional hiccup.

More calves continued to arrive about every seven weeks, but the third lot consisted of only four calves which were not sufficient for my needs, so I had another eight from John Yarnold, however a couple of these were so large having been with the cows for so long that they proved to be "Buggers to get to drink". I persevered and succeeded in the end.

Heather changed schools after the summer holidays and started at Tenbury Wells High School.

Jim Gough, John's brother, seemed to acquire a race horse for himself, rumour had it over a pint !!! After getting it home he didn't know what to do with it, so he came to see my mother, who agreed to keep it at the Mount. At first we put the racehorse out with Silver, as we had done all the fencing around her field, then all went well until the racehorse was taken away for training, and as Rosie would have to be taken out of the field shortly being due to calf again I thought I had better find a companion for Silver pronto.

I hitched a lift into Hereford again, and purchased a Welsh Black bullock, for which I paid £70, getting him home on the lorry owned by Jones, High House Farm, in which I also got a lift. The bullock was christened "Wog" and he and Silver settled down, and Rosie was taken out of the field when her calf was born in September. She had a heifer calf, which I reared on the bucket alongside the contract calves, taking her off Rosie when she was a week old and Rosie was then able to join the other two once more.

We continued to rear calves for the Bishops. I recall that a calf in one batch kept on blowing , we tried all methods including putting oil down, piping and eventually John Gough came down, and poured a solution of salt water into the calf, we could see that he was still blowing, so John got his pen knife and put a slit in the stomach and out came 'North Sea Gas!!!" That cured it but only for a short time, it continued to be a problem, however we were able to send it back to the Bishops at twelve weeks as normal.

Another problem, a calf seen by the vet, seemed to thrive but kept going up and down, when eventually he died after he had been returned to the Bishop's they noticed that he had a lump in his throat and found that a blockage in the throat had been causing all his problems.

Builders by the name of Hadcock got the contract to split our house The Mount into two dwellings. My parents decided on this approach as the house was large and needed a great deal of money spent on it to complete the renovations, and this seemed the best option.

The builders began in the summer of 1972. The original house was L shaped and we began by blocking off the front from the side wing. This entailed blocking off three doors to make them separate units. The front now being a viable unit was put up for sale. In the wing that we retained for our home, a hop drying room was converted into three bedrooms, this now gave us a total of four bedrooms in our unit. In addition we had a dining room, kitchen and bathroom.

The front unit was bought by Warwick and Jenny Gledhill, who moved to the area from Huddersfield. Mr. Gledhill was a commercial traveller.

The new year came and on 1st. January 1973 Britain became a member of the E.E.C. - European Economic Community.

I continued to rear my calves getting them mainly from John Yarnold, the calf dealer who lived just a mile away, and when the calves were weaned they were bought by the Bishops 'for Rearing on'.

I purchased during April at a Russell, Baldwin, and Bright machinery sale in Hereford a Mayfield Mower, which cost £25, and Morris Bufton Auctioneers from Ludlow, kindly dropped myself and the mower home. This machine was a great asset as I could now go round the field, and keep it topped, bringing in mown grass every other day for mum to use for the horses.

Mum sold one of her ponies for a good price during the month, and put the proceeds towards the purchase of a Land Rover and trailer, from a Mr Sparrow. The Land Rover had a current M.O.T. however, shortly afterwards Dad heard a thumping from the wheels, and asked Lex Meade in Hereford just to check it out before they put the hitch on, and to my parents horror, it was discovered that the wheel hubs had been welded on and it took 3 months and £1100 to get it put right.

Rupert got married at the end of May. He and Jill (his new wife) moving to live near Heathrow, as at the end of the previous year Rupert had obtained a new job as an Immigration Officer at the airport.

During the year we worked on our half of the original garden. Putting down a new lawn, but retaining part of the old vegetable garden, we now had a rotovator, and this was a great help in the cultivation department.

Mum, Dad and Heather, went for a few days holiday in Angelsey visiting friends, and also taking Jerry, one of the ponies to a showing class at the Angelsey Show. Heather would ride the pony on these occasions and we were often in the prize money.

In August the half of the calf unit which Dad had been using as a workshop, while I built up my calf enterprise, was again incorporated in the main unit. This meant that I could now rear twenty calves at a time, instead of the batches of twelve I had been rearing. This being the case twenty calves were installed during August, and these kept me mighty busy!!

At the beginning of September the vet put an implant in the ear of Silver which contained ' Growth Hormones' as I wanted to show him at the Christmas show in Kidderminster.

I sold 'Wog' at the beginning of October to 'Bowketts' in Tenbury Wells and he made £192, minus £2 which they deducted for the transport.

At the end of October I was ready for my second batch of twenty calves. I kept 'Silver' in a loose box from October letting him out into the field for approximately half an hour while I cleaned out his box.

Mum's friend, Mary Creed went to Australia for six months, and during that time her son Tim who was nearly seventeen, stayed with us, plus their dog, a Great Dane called 'Twinkle' fortunately he got on well with our dogs!!!

In November we had quite a lot of sharp frosts, and our pond froze over, sufficiently for Tim to be pulled across the ice by 'Twinkle' who had his pullover in a firm grip in his mouth It looked so funny, fortunately the ice was thick enough to take their weight.

As the Fatstock Show was to be held on Tuesday 11th December. I was busy, when not involved with the calves, getting Silver into tiptop condition. A reporter from the 'Worcester Evening News' came out to our home and took a photograph of Silver and myself a few days before the fatstock show. The day arrived and we borrowed Philip Gough's lorry, Mum and I loaded Silver up, and trundelled along to the market with high hopes. There were a great many people and a lot of stock present, and although we didn't get a prize a great many people complimented me on Silver's turn out, and we had a very enjoyable day.

Although Dad took Mr Sparrow to Court over the Land Rover he had purchased from him. He was very disappointed to be only awarded £40, a mere drop in the ocean considering what it had cost to put the Land Rover right, and before the end of the year he decided to get rid of it, and purchased a lorry, which he converted into a horse box.

Our Christmas turkey that year came from the 'Bishops' our calf rearing contractors, as they also reared turkeys.

1974 came and the Bishops decided that they didn't want to continue putting calves in for rearing so David Knowsworthy a contractor who did our hedging decided that he would provide me with a batch of twenty to rear on.

He therefore went down to Carmarthan market, with a neighbour to purchase the necessary calves. Twenty Fresian bull calves, were delivered, and out of that batch I successfully reared all but one.

When these calves were weaned and moved, another batch arrived from David Knowsworthy. These calves were Hereford/Cross, I really only had room for twenty calves, but due to David's neighbour not realising, and purchasing another eight on their behalf, I ended up with a batch of twenty eight - managing to find the odd corners in which to rear the extra calves.

The original Fresian calves left our premises for rearing on.

As calf prices were so poor David Knosworthy decided that it wasn't worth putting any more calves through until prices improved, especially as you could buy weaned calves at the same prices as week old calves. Yet again I trundelled into Hereford on a Wednesday, and placed yet another advert for Contract Calf Rearing. Ring Newnham Bridge 391. At the same time I let it be known in the market that I was on the lookout for good Charolais calves for my own personal rearing.

The Friday evening at about 6p.m. brought a response to my advert when a Mr. Capper telephoned from Burley Gate near Hereford. It was arranged that he and his wife would come out to see my calf rearing set up. He was obviously impressed by what he saw, because he arranged for twenty calves to be delivered the following Wednesday. Additionally, he provided scales as he wanted to weigh the calves as they came off the lorry, so that he had a note of their delivery weights for M.L.C. record purposes.

When the calves arrived on a lorry driven by Mr. Harris and his son they proved to be quite whoppers of calves some nearly too large for the pens, and almost ready for weaning. Mr. Capper also provided the milk powder, hay, straw and calf nuts. However some of these calves wouldn't drink, and just threw their calf nuts all over the place, we persevered and eventually managed to rear all the calves.to weaning etc. One of this batch I recall did have us up most of one night when he got blown, Mr. Capper wanted us to use his own vets from Leominster, and so a Mr. Newt came out and cut the calf to reduce its blown state. Mr. Capper had by now appointed a new stockman Mervyn Lake and he came over and dehorned the calves at six weeks.

I had by now obtained three Charolais calves of my own which I was rearing in addition to the contract calves.

Mr. Cappers calves were finally moved into the weaned pen, and then it was back to the start again, more muscle and muck, cleaning out and disinfecting the pens ready for a new batch of calves.

Morgan Edwards came to mow our field for hay, but infuriatingly it was just making well when the rainy season started, and so unfortunately we had a disappointing result. I decided to mow the bank to the field, which was too steep for the mower, with a Mayfield Scythe, although it only made 11 bales of hay, which David Knosworthy (Nossy) baled, it really tidied up the field.

A further twenty calves were were delivered on contract for Mr. Capper, at the end of July and these did O.K. About the middle of August, Mr. Capper took away the first batch of weaned calves, and I was quite relieved as some of them were getting to be a problem to keep in the pen as they were so large!! Reg was the lorry driver who always carried Mr.Cappers calves

As usual all the pens had to be prepared after moving the second batch of calves on into the weaning pen, and we were ready for the third batch of calves about the middle of September. Melvyn Lake came over weekly, bringing the feed rations, and discussing any problems.

After the third batch Mr. Capper decided that he didn't want any more calves reared away from his premises, so that ended rearing for Mr. Capper for a while.

Meanwhile, my own three Charolais calves continued to grow well, and by this time were out in the field happily grazing.

In went the advert again for "Contract calf rearing" in the Hereford Times.

Although a close neighbour wanted some calves reared it would not be for a month or so, therefore I accepted a Mr. Meredith from the Brecon area. Due to the distance he did not come out to check the pens, and simply arrived with twenty calves loaded on a trailer pulled by a Land Rover.

They settled in well and were no trouble to get drinking etc. They were weaned after Christmas and as Mr. Meredith only wanted me to take them to seven weeks, he returned in January 1975, and took them away. I was then ready to rear for my close neighbour David Spillsbury. John Yarnold was the calf dealer acting for him, and unfortunately was supplying the calves in dribs and drabs two or three at a time, until we had a batch of twenty. This was not good from my point of view as the rearer, particularly, as Mum went into a newly arrived calf that looked O.K., a minute later it barked and then kicked the bucket. This batch proved to be trouble, trouble, trouble.!!!

In fact we only lost one but, we had virus pneumonia in the batch, and new calves coming into this atmosphere quickly succumbed to the virus. We had to have a lot of vet visits, in fact it got so bad at one stage that we were thinking of telling John Yarnold to take all the calves away. however we struggled on, but were very thankful to see that batch leave at twelve weeks fully weaned.

After the usual cleaning and disinfecting of the pens, we were ready for another batch and Ron Meredith wanted me to put another batch through for him. Meanwhile I sold one of my Charolais bullocks and purchased two more calves for my personal rearing.

At the same time I had been asked if I could rear seven poor runty looking calves which were owned by Mr. Capper's stockman, he had been allowed to keep and rear these independent of his job, but Mr. Capper's Manager didn't want these animals on the farm, so I took them, and put them separate to my contract calves into two adjacent looses boxes.

Elizabeth, my eldest sister, was now at Hereford College of Art, and Heather still at the High School in Tenbury.

Father was now working in Worcester with a Mental Health Rehabilitation unit. This involved helping people who had come out of mental institutions adapt again to a life in the community. He was working on a shift system as these people needed twenty four hour supervision.

Mum continued to help me with the calves and in addition she schooled horses. We had at this time Flash, a pony that Heather rode in showing classes, winning a number of prizes for the owner Anne Colbatch-Clarke from Canon Pyon.

I took my two big Charolais beef into Kidderminster at the end of May. One weighed 9 1/2 cwt. and made £215, and the other weighed 8 cwt. and made £160. I had to let them go at this time, as I was very short of grass.

I had a further batch from Ron Meredith in June, these proved to be O.K. June that year was very hot and that proved to be the start of a very mild winter and exceptionally hot summer in 1976.

The grass was cut for hay and this year we had a really good crop and made about 110 bales.

Bryan and Mays owned the estate next door to the "Mount" and in August they had straw for sale, after the fields had been combined. David Spillsbury wanted some straw, we wanted a bit so it was agreed that "Nossy" would do the baling. I took enough to fill the loft.

About September I had another batch for David Spillsbury, John Yarnold supplied the calves again, but in a couple of bunches, we were not having the fiasco of the first time!!! These proved to be no problem and so six weeks later it was back to more muscle and muck.

A further batch followed from David Spillsbury, and the last batch that I reared in 1975 were put in by Edward Gough, and with the exception of one little runt of a calf which wouldn't drink, they proved to be reasonable bunch to rear.

However David Spillsbury's calves caught pneumonia after they were weaned and in the loose pen, just days before they should have left, we therefore had to keep them on unfortunately until they were clear, and regrettably one did not recover and we lost it.

Rosie, our house cow, sadly had to be put down by the vet as she had a dislocated shoulder, mastitis, and a bulge on her eye, and as she was obviously suffering we had to let her go.

At about the same time an aged pony that we had been looking after and had reached thirty plus years also had to be put down.

At the beginning of January 1976, on an evening that Dad, Mum, a cousin and Heather attended a play at Dad's work place in Worcester, we had a tremendous gale. In fact the roof blew off the garage. Inside the garage was a colleague of Dad's car, who had recently emigrated to Australia. Although the car was O.K. you couldn't get at it as the roof had come down over the doors!!! At that time we had a Great Dane called Valley, she asked to go out, but I think that she was so frightened by the storm that she stood 'frozen to the ground' for about half an hour before returning.

My parents managed to get back safely, and the next day we surveyed the damage. We had to jack up the garage roof, to get the weight off the doors, get the car out and then repair the roof.

The calf pens needed cleaning but yet again, and I had 20 of Mr. Cappers Hereford/Fresian heifer calves,. They arrived on February 2nd and there was about six inches of snow on the ground, consequently Mr Harris the driver couldn't get the lorry up the 'Bank' so he had to lead each calf up to the pens separately, this, took a little while, but at least all the calves were safely installed.

These calves went on O.K. and then after five to six weeks it was like 'Musical Chairs' moving stock around to create space in the weaning pens. Thankfully Edward Gough's calves went back alright.

Michael Morgan another local farmer wanted some calves rearing so I did two batches for him. The first batch were some Continental and Fresian Hereford Cross, and these went on to a Mr. Knott the 'Hop Farm' near Tenbury Wells. The second batch were Fresians and these went back to Michael Morgan after they were weaned.

Meanwhile I bought four Fresian/ Hereford/Charolais Cross calves for my own personal rearing, and the two beasts who had been out in the field I sold. They weighed eight and a half cwt. and made £250 each.

During the very hot weather of the summer of 1976, I was kept very busy with all the calves.

In addition to the usual batch of 20, I had two small loose boxes with five calves in each. It was not ideal, but I did it as a favour to Chris Janes who wanted a few calves reared. Thank goodness having taken the risk to rear these without individual pens they came in and they went out O.K.

Phil Morgan, a calf dealer, called one Sunday evening towards the end of June, to ask if I would consider rearing a batch of calves for veal. I had them for five weeks, and during this time the liquid only feed had to build up to a gallon in the morning, and a further gallon in the evening. Regrettably I lost five partly due to the weather conditions as it was so hot and humid. When the remaining calves left my premises they went to Gatwick airport to be flown to Italy.

Conditions were so dry that summer that our pond dried up and great cracks appeared in the silt. The four calves that I owned were out in the field, and one seeking shade from the sun went into the dried up pond and sank into the silt - fortunately we managed to get him out with some verbal encouragement.

We made 300 odd bales of hay that summer. After the veal calves went I had a massive cleaning task on hand, much greater than after putting the usual batches through. Again in 1976, David Knosworthy (Nossy) baled straw for us from Bryant and Mays land at the Lodge next door. Although it was a fifty acre field the corn had been grown in strips with barren land in between. I found that it was best in such hot weather to start at 5 a.m. see to the calves and then have a siesta in the middle of the day, before continuing after the fiercest heat was beginning to recede.

At the end of August I had a DAYS HOLIDAY. My parents and Heather were going to Angelsey for a summer break and I joined them for a day. I spent the day sunbathing and swimming in the sea. On my return journey, Guess What? It started to rain, and so began a period of decidedly wet weather, which continued to be greater than usual until the following March 1977. A farming neighbour called Les Gittins, who had farmed in the area for the past four years, wanted a batch reared and these Hereford Cross calves brought me real trouble in the form of Salmonella.

At about the same time I could see that my four bullocks were going downhill, so Les Gittins drenched them for worms, and fortunately this cleared the problem.

Regrettably I lost five calves from Les Gittins batch in spite of a number of visits from the vet. After these calves had been weaned, I again cleared out cleaned and disinfected the pens, leaving them empty for a couple of weeks, before introducing any more calves into the calf house. Mr. Capper wanted some more calves reared, and I felt that after such a hot summer and intensive rearing this was advisable.

When Mr. Harrisons brother came to deliver Mr Cappers calves after helping me to put them in the pens, he returned to his drivers cab in the lorry and handed down a large Cheddar cheese for the family to enjoy.

In November I bought three Charolais calves for my own rearing.

Christmas was fast approaching and I was nice and busy with calves which were going well. Les Gittins calves went back before Christmas and the weather over the Christmas period was dry and not too cold. We had a nice family Christmas, with Rupert and his wife returning for the occasion.

I moved the calves into the weaning pens in January 1977, and then Guess What? Yes, it was time for me to muck out again!!!! A further batch were sent in on behalf of Mr. Capper, unfortunately this batch had a touch of pneumonia, which necessitated a visit from the vet, and this is when I first met John Bell, a young vet who had recently joined the Leominster Practice, coming from up north (Geordie land I think) The pneumonia cleared up and the rearing then proceeded at a more satisfactory pace.

Reg, Mr.Capper's haulage driver, came and collected the batches of calve's, as they were ready.

Towards the end of April and beginning of May we had a lot of very strong and drying winds. During this time Dad and I had to take a pony up to Cumbria, managing to do the return journey in a day. We noticed that a trailer which had been parked at the top of the bank in the field had been blown a fair way down the bank, fortunately stopped from getting blown any further by a railway sleeper, which was lying on the ground.

I purchased a further three Charolais calves for my own rearing at the end of April.

Morgan Edwards mowed the field for hay, turned the hay, and then the heavens opened and it rained for four to five weeks with no break long enough to get near the hay, a ruined crop was the result!! A relation of Morgan came and baled it, and took it away, it was all black and musty. Fortunately having got the rubbish hay off the grass grew sufficiently to get off.

I did three batches for Michael Morgan, and then it was back to a further three batches for Mr. Capper.

I sold the three small Charolais at the end of September, and the three large ones a couple of weeks later as they kept breaking out of their field. Out of the proceeds I purchased a further three Charolais calves for my own rearing. Towards the end of November I put them into a ventilated loose box and they did O.K. Feeding was always mad with the three all wanting to feed from the bucket first.

We put another loose box up attached to the garage, which gave me further facilities for the calves. I found it easier to feed them this way, in a smaller loose box, as the calves got older and larger it was easier to stop them charging around than in the larger loose boxes.

In retrospect 1977 was a busy but uneventful year, there were the usual ups and downs but nothing dramatic.

In the Spring of 1978 Michael Morgan, who lived about a mile and a half away, wanted me to rear some calves for a Mr. Knott, that he knew well. This was followed by another batch for Michael Morgan, and then a batch for Jim Gough. We were getting to the middle of the year and it was becoming difficult to get batches to rear.

I kept on hitching into Kidderminster for the Tuesday market and

Hereford for the Wednesday market, looking up old contact and hoping that someone would know of somebody who required calves rearing. Fortunately, eventually through a friend of a friend of a friend!! I heard of a Mr. Price from south of Hereford who wanted calves reared, only problem was they were to be reared for veal, not my preference, but needs must and I undertook to rear them. I had them for about five weeks when they had to be able to take a gallon of milk in the morning and a further gallon of milk in the evening. as usual some were easy to feed and some very difficult. After feeding them for the last time I said HOORAY! and John Yarrnold collected them and delivered them to Mr. Prices premises on a Wednesday.

I had extra cleaning problems after the veal calves and had just got everything shipshape and was wondering what I was going to do, and where the next batch was coming from when Mr. Capper's Farm Manager John Llewellyn rang up and said "Could I manage to do a batch of calves." Heaven sent, just as I was getting desperate.

Apparently my good fortune was as a result of Mr Capper's Head Stockmans misfortune. The latter had apparently been walking home in thick fog after ringing the church bells. He thought he was walking along a path but was actually on the top of a wall from which he fell injuring himself badly and breaking his hip This resulted in him being in hospital about six weeks.

My parents put pressure on me to get rid of at least one of the bullocks that I was rearing as they were poaching the field so I entered him in Hereford market where he made a reasonably good price.

The winter of 1978 was very nasty and cold seeming to go on for a long time. During that time I reared a further two batches for Mr. Capper which took me into early 1979. When they were ready to go into the larger pen we had to take each calf the long way round through ice and snow, as we had stored hay in the area which would have given us a shorter route. This meant that each calf had to be led round, and in some cases it took the three of us, ie. Mum, Dad, and myself to get them round, with two pulling and one pushing. What a performance as some of the calves were quite large.

Winter seemed never ending, but with animals depending on me, it was a case of shutting up and getting on with it, and there was always the great feeling, when all work was done, of returning to the house, and being free to soak up the warmth. I didn't have any modern feeding methods, and it was a case of filling the calf buckets from a trough, some would inevitably get spilt, and in the freezing cold weather ice would form, which would add to my problems, as I slipped and slid to get the job done.

Spring gradually approached, and as the weather improved I forgot the worst rigours of the winter.

My two beasts had overwintered well and they were now about eighteen months old, and had feet as large as fire bucket especially if they stood on you, fortunately they didn't do that too often.

I did another batch of calves for Michael Morgan, they did alright. Followed by another batch of veal calves for Mr. Price. I disliked doing calves for veal but needs must and I would rather have been working than twiddling my thumbs, and it kept the old cash flow going.

I bought hay from Morgan Edwards as it was so convenient, when he was bailing hay in fields so close to our house.

I did a batch of calves for Mr. Capper. They came in toward, the end of July/August. These were followed by a batch for S.L.P. (Shropshire Livestock Producers) I heard about the latter, the usual way via the market, meeting a friend who worked for Russell, Baldwin and Bright the auctioneers. He telephoned an acquaintance on my behalf, and I agreed to go and see their representative in offices close to the market. The outcome was a batch of calves to rear, but I had to provide all the food. I was willing to give it a go. The calves came directly from their birth farms to a lorry which collected from farm to farm, and then delivered them directly to myself the rearer. This way they didn't go near the market, and the reduced level of stress and risk of infection was therefore minimal. As a result this proved to be a fairly trouble free batch to rear. Also a chap called Peter Hamilton, who did the organising for S.L.P. would pop in fairly regularly to see if there were any problems I needed to discuss. I found that providing the food myself made the final costing work out slightly to my disadvantage.

This batch proved to be the only batch that I reared for S.L.P. as following these Mr. Capper required a further two batches.

I started additional feeding for my two beasts from about the end of August, and brought them inside, housing them in a loose box from the beginning of October, with the aim of entering them into the Banbury Christmas Fatstock Show I was told about this being a good market for my beasts by contacts, who would also be in a position, to help me with transport.

I continued to feed them on rolled barley, and endeavoured to keep my feet out of the way of their feet at feeding time!! Knowing that my two beasts would shortly be going, I purchased three more Charolais calves for my own private rearing.

Prior to the big day of the Fatstock market. I gave both beasts a good grooming, and they looked quite good and clean, when they were loaded onto the lorry on the evening before the market. I sat in the cab with the driver, the firm was Bates of Kidderminster.

It took us a couple of hours to get there and I unloaded my beasts into an allocated pen. I was invited by some of the auctioneers staff to the pub for a meal and a drink or two. The night was spent on the floor of the auctioneers office! It was a bit hard but I managed.

Wednesday morning dawned, and I set too grooming and giving the two beasts a bit of spit and polish I was only actually showing one in the ring and that proved to be a bit of a problem as the beast did not want to be led, fortunately someone came and helped me lead, holding the animals head on the opposite side.

Regrettably no prizes were won by my beasts, but it all proved to be an enjoyable experience. The evening found me back in the pub for another meal, followed by a further night on the floor of the auctioneers office. The next day, Thursday was fatstock day, both beasts were sold. They each made 81p a kilo, and as they weighed 14 and 15 cwt. respectively I was not disappointed.

I hitch hiked to Shrewsbury for the first time, just on an impulse one Friday when I did not have a great deal of work on. I decided that I would visit the physiotherapist at the Royal Shrewsbury Hospital who had worked so hard with me, Miss Bloor. It was now twenty one years since my accident falling off the bicycle. Miss Bloor was very pleased to see me, and after visiting I was able to get a lift on the return journey from just south of Shrewsbury, followed fairly rapidly by a further lift home, making the journey in good time to do the evening feeding rounds for the animals.

After returning home from the fatstock show in Banbury, after things had settled down, I set to cleaning out the loose box which had housed the two beasts while I was fattening them prior to the show. Special cleaning was required as it was the intention to turn this building into a house. Odd to think that ten years ago this was the first building that Dad and I converted to take the first batch of calves that I reared at the "Mount".

A builder was employed to convert this building into a house, adding a further wing, and altering the loft to make bedroom accommodation I was not going to be involved as I was too busy with my animals.

The intention was that as the family accommodation needs had altered now that Rupert was married, Elizabeth to be married shortly, and Heather who had just completed a two year Domestic Science course at a college in Worcester and was about to take a post with horses on the Lancashire/Yorkshire border, would be greatly reduced. As a result a much smaller house would now be adequate for our needs, and my parents decided, that when the conversion was completed we would move in and sell our present abode.

Losing the large loose box made life more difficult for me. It wasn t so bad when the calves first came in but as they grew and I had to utilise the less convenient loose boxes, it made for greater distances between the boxes and all the doors had to be constantly washed down to keep muck off them and enable them to close easily.

Unfortunately during the loose box conversion period in May of 1980 Heather fractured her collar bone, and came home to recuperate. My parents took her back up to the local hospital close to her job one day to keep an appointment, and it was about 10.30a.m when I heard the most terrifying crash, thinking about it now makes me shudder.

The Gable end of the building that was being converted just collapsed and fell to the ground. Father had already drawn the builders attention to a crack which had appeared in a wall that was being rebuilt, but they didn't appear to take any notice, and went ahead and removed the scaffolding, mainly I think because they wanted it for another job that they were doing, building a grain silo at the Lodge close by.

When my parents rang from away I said that there had been bit of a disaster with the building, I didn't elaborate, in order not to worry them further, but it left me shaking for hours, and recalling this event it still makes me shudder.

Muggins got the job of helping clear up some of the mess, which was necessary anyway, in order for me to get round my calves.

Tim shrugs off sickness with a smile

THE WORLD fell apart for Mr and Mrs John Montgomery the day their seven-year-old son Timothy was involved in an accident.

He was found with head injuries by the side of a Shropshire road and the bicycle he had been riding was on the ground beside him. For three months, Tim lay unconscious in the Midland Neuro-Surgery Hospital at Smethwick.

He was eventually discharged without speech, paralysed on his right side and possibly blind in one eye. Doctors said he was lucky to be alive.

While a boy, Timothy underwent a number of operations to improve his eyesight and body movements at hospitals in Hereford, Oswestry and Shrewsbury. They were successful, but when he left school, Tim was rated as being "unemployable."

'CABBAGE'

However, he was not prepared to accept the sort of life which lay before him —that of a "written-off cabbage."

The date of the road accident is one that Timothy is never likely to forget: January 3, 1958.

Now aged 23, he lives with his family at Rochford Mount, near Tenbury Wells. He limps slightly, speaks slowly, has a keen sense of humour, sees things very much in perspective and has proved the authorities wrong. Tim is not unemployable.

Two years ago, he hitch-hiked over 30 miles to Hereford market and returned home with a Charolais/Friesian bull calf named Silver, which he intended to rear.

When he first brought Silver home, his parents weren't too sure he would be able to cope, but a building at the back of the house was utilised for the calf and tomorrow the bullock is being entered at Kidderminster Prize Show and Sale. Tim is hoping that Silver can take one of the prizes.

"I've always been interested in farming and used to help on a farm just up the road," he said. "Before I had Silver I bought another calf from Tenbury market and later sold him for quite a good price."

Tim has a dogged determination to succeed where others said he would certainly fail.

In a further effort to utilise the calf house, and quite unknown to his parents, he advertised to rear calves on a contract basis. The first batch of 20 calves have just passed successfully through his hands.

Tim gives injections to sick calves, sees to 99 per cent of their welfare and is a match for their bull strength anytime.

"I look after the calves for three months, feed them, muck them out and turn them out loose. I hope the contracts will prove quite profitable," he added.

Mr and Mrs Montgomery have obviously had worries about their son. "But we have found he has determination and he really does sort his own problems out," said his father.

"It's not a bad effort for a supposedly unemployable young man. I'm sure Tim can encourage all handicapped persons to soldier on."

Tim Montgomery with his Charolais-Freisian bullock "Silver".

© Shropshire Star

Two Feet and a Thumb

The hitch-hiker's guide to full life

Tim Montgomery was a healthy seven-year-old when a tragic accident left him severely disabled.

But this has not deterred him from leading a full and active life.

Now, at 30, he spends his working day rearing calves and in his spare time he hitch-hikes to the surrounding cattle markets.

Tim was on his way to post a Christmas thank-you letter on January 3, 1958, when his cycle skidded on ice near his then Ratlinghope home near Bishop's Castle.

He was thrown to the ground and bumped his head which resulted in a fractured skull and three months in a coma.

This affected his speech and movements and left him partially paralysed.

During his schooldays, spent at a special school near Coventry, he learned to cope with his disability.

Combined with the support of his parents this meant he can now lead a full and active life.

His day starts just after 6 a.m. at the home he shares with his parents, The Coach House, in Upper Rochford, near Tenbury Wells.

After feeding and tending his 40 calves he hitches to the nearby cattle markets when a sale is being held.

Public transport is a problem in this outlying area which makes hitch-hiking essential for Tim who cannot drive.

Tim started hitch-hiking 10 years ago and says he now gets lifts regularly from the people who first stopped for him several years ago.

© Worcester Evening News

The long and winding road for Tim Montgomery of Rochford, near Tenbury Wells.

Hitch-hiker Timothy is uplifted

TIMOTHY MONTGOMERY is arguably Herefordshire's leading authority on hitch-hiking.

For every fortnight for the past 10 years he has hitched the 28 miles from his home at Rochford, near Tenbury to Hereford cattle market.

Timothy, aged 31, rears calves under contract to other farmers on his six acre small-holding at Rochford and likes to keep in touch with the cattle trade.

But because of a childhood accident which left him disabled he is unable to drive and relies on the goodwill of motorists for a ride.

"Sometimes I have a terrible job getting a lift. I may wait an hour or the best part of a day but the secret is to be patient," said Timothy.

It's a virtue he needs in abundance. For Timothy also regularly hitches the 23 miles to Kidderminster cattle market.

He said: "I like to see what trade is like and meet other people in the same business."

Timothy Montgomery hitching a lift home after a sale in Hereford Market.

I also scraped a great many bricks clean of mortar as they were to be reused.

One of my calves I'm sure suffered from all the dust, that was created when the building collapsed, as he subsequently showed asthma like symptoms, along with a virus pneumonia, it appeared to clear, and then would flare up again. Mr. Capper's stockman Phil Prees who came over periodically to see if there were any problems, and bring over the feed decided to take the calf off my hands, back to Lower Hope Farm. I subsequently heard that he was alright for 4/5 weeks, had a further attack and then died.

The building recommenced, but that was by no means the last of our problems. The builders and electricians didn't see eye to eye, and eventually Dad told Haywoods the builders either to get on and finish the job, as they kept leaving the site for other work, or clear off, as we had had nothing but trouble for months. The builders chose to leave. As a result builder friends of ours called George's completed the building.

Mum and Dad and any of the family who happened by did the decorating, so eventually we ended up with a three bedroomed house that we called the "Coach House".

Meanwhile I had purchased a further two calves Fresian/Charolais for my own personal rearing from part of the profits of my Banbury Cattle sale.

I carried on rearing calves throughout 1980. I made another contact with a chap I had met occasionally at farm sales or the market, he was called Alfie Morgan, and he decided to put a batch in with me towards the end of that year. They were mainly small Fresian/Hereford Heifer calves. I had a few problems, touch of pneumonia here and there, but they came in and went out, and anyway Alfie was pleased so that was the most important.

The big day came, Moving day, December 18th, it was a Thursday, and the weather fortunately was very mild. All hands were needed to lift furniture etc. across. I remember now that this was just ten days after John Lennon, one of the Beatles, was shot in New York, and how everyone gasped at the news.

We moved the basic things into the house, but as the new people who had bought our old house the "Mount" were not moving in until January, I took advantage of this situation and continued to mix up the milk powder for the calves in our old kitchen.

The new people duly arrived in January, a Mr. & Mrs.Fish and their three children. We had put up a dividing wall between the two properties so each was now self contained.

I carried on with my calf rearing during 1981, mainly for Mr. Capper who provided me with steady work in regular batches of calves. We didn't aim to do any improvements to the buildings that year as we were all recovering from the major house building project of the year before.

Prince Charles tied the knot with Lady Diana on the 19th July, and in between calf feedings I watched the proceedings on the television, along with the rest of the nation.

I did the usual buying of hay from my neighbours when it was being baled by a contractor. I continued to churn calves out for Mr. Capper and then Alfie Morgan put me in touch with a new contact from Rhayader, who wanted calves rearing towards the end of November, this meant a very busy period, as my own two beasts were to be entered into the Kidderminster Fatstock Show. I was pleased with the latter they had done well, although they were slightly smaller than my last fat cattle being about 15 cwt.

I set about the usual pre-show spit and polish, and it was arranged that Jones, Haulage from Upper Sapey would transport myself and the beasts to the show. We were all ready to go when it began to SNOW.

A quick wizard blizzard fell and instead of getting to the market by 10.30 am as anticipated, due to having about 8" of snow, and very slippery conditions it was 11.30 a.m. Most people had been held up by the adverse weather, and the start of the market had been delayed as a result. Again, it was not my luck to be amongst the prizewinners, but I was pleased with the way the beasts sold for reasonably good prices.

Fortunately Mum and Heather came to pick me up and I was very grateful as it was blooming cold. We got home safely, winter had really started with a vengeance. It was hard to keep the calves water buckets free of ice.

Just before Christmas there was a further fall of snow, and the family took advantage of this to go sledging. Rupert, coming down the hill on the sledge hit a hidden mole hill, and parted from the sledge injuring his pride and getting a bruised bottom. I caught the flu. It continued to be good sledging weather for a few days, but I concentrated on just feeding my calves and nursing my bout of flu, trying to keep myself warm.

The thaw came just after Christmas but this was followed by yet another wizard blizzard. Bernie who lived just at the top of the hill from the Coach House, on returning from the pub, fell into a snow drift, and was shovelled up by the snow plough. Rumour had it that he would not have died of hypothermia as he had so much alcohol inside him.!!!!

The snow was a really nice dry compact variety, which wouldn't make snow balls, but was crisp to walk on, a pleasant change from all the wet stuff we usually got. (It was so cold that the milk froze as soon as it left the cow).

It was so far below freezing that when I was feeding the calves, and pouring their milk into the buckets, (you could not possibly wear gloves, as they would be permanently wet with milk spills) it was difficult to keep my fingers functioning, and additionally very difficult to keep the calves water buckets free from ice.

The calves I had in at that time were being reared for a Mr. Thomas from Rhayader, and inspite of the cold weather and the usual ups and downs the batch did quite well. These were followed by a further batch from Mr. Capper, and then in the spring of 1982 it was decided to erect a new calf house.

Dad bought a second hand tractor, a Dexter 1964, for general use around the farm, and to help with preparing the base for the new calf building. I would have liked to have driven the tractor, but Dad always insisted on doing the driving. It was a very tight squeeze around the buildings, no doubt Dad thought that I might not clear the corners!!!

Dad got contractors in to level the ground and put down chippings to form a base for the new calf house. We planned to construct a building which would contain 28 individual calf pens, and additionally lean to calf boxes to take calves on after they were weaned, on the other building.

We had by now purchased a cement mixer, thanks to me spotting it in a private sale. I felt even better at getting it for £40 rather than the asking price of £65. Yipee, no more mixing concrete by hand. Percy, who worked for Georges the builders did the concreting and put up the internal brickwork. Initially we had no trouble, but then the concrete mixer kept stopping. Apparently we needed a new plug. Mum went down to Tenbury to try and purchase one and was advised to try Geoffery Buckingham Bowden at the nursery, where she was successful, result one happy cement mixer and even happier people

Mr. Davies a constructional engineer erected the building. I already had 20 pens to transfer from another building, and we purchased a further 12 to complete the building and have a few spare.

Returning home from Hereford a local farmer and councillor Mr. Terry James gave me a lift all the way home one day, and decided that he would like me to rear some calves for him. These calves proved to be the last to be reared in the old buildings, and the second batch I reared for him, were the first to be reared in the new calf house.

It was wonderful working in the spacious new building, although the pens remained the same size, the passageways etc. were much larger.

In 1983 we put on a small meal/mixing lean-to, this meant that I could mix up the milk powder, and had the calves meal all adjacent to the rearing pens. What bliss I now had everything to hand. After eleven years of walking from the kitchen in our original house "The Mount", where I used to mix the milk powder, to the calf house, carrying twenty pints of milk, twice over, morning and evening. Is it any wonder that I have got long arms.

That year we had a very hot summer, and the calf house with every pen filled, really proved how efficient a purpose built building can prove. It was well ventilated, kept reasonably cool, and consequently didn't get invaded by flies, which used to be such a problem in the previous set up.

After weaning the calves, we put them into the small loose boxes. Five calves to each box putting a hurdle across each of the individual boxes so that we could leave the doors open at each end of the building, to keep the ventilation at the maximum during the heat.

Now that we lived at the Coach House, we had a greatly reduced garden. Just a lawn, pond, and flower beds. We no longer had room for a vegetable plot (that I hated working on anyway - although I didn't mind the harvesting part).

Mum helped me with the calves, doing all the drenching, and giving of the injections. She found it a considerable help being long legged in anchoring the calves.

Mr. Capper was next to put a batch through in the new building, but as his system was geared to 20 calves at a time it left me with 8 spare pens which I couldn't fill in case it caused cross infection. This latest batch from Mr. Capper made it 500 calves that I had reared for him since I started, and during that period I had only lost 3 calves, the former all proving to be really topping calves.

Mr. Cappers stockman came round to dehorn the calves, before leaving his position with the former. While he was talking to my mother and self, he said that there were rumours that Mr. Capper was thinking of selling his farming estate. This was a big shock for me, as he had been my most consistent supplier of calves.

The rumours proved to be true. However it was decided that I should do a couple more batches, as it would take time for the sale to go through.

As I still continued to do my hitch hiking to Kidderminster and Hereford markets, one day I met a chap who said that he knew of a person who wanted calves rearing. The latter contacted me and came over to see my set up. He was most impressed and we made a deal on behalf of Hinwoods from Cleobury Mortimer.

That brought us to Sept./Oct. 1983. The calves arrived in small groups, but they drank well and did O.K. We repeated the usual pattern, weaning and putting them into the loose boxes in small groups, ready to leave us at twelve weeks.

As rearing calves was a twice a day job seven days a week, it left very little time, if any for outside interests. In the better weather I usually walked the dogs in the evening, usually up towards the Lodge, and then along the lanes for as far as I wished to walk. At that time we had a whippet called Slipper who belonged to Mum, and a Great Dane called Valley.

Mum had made a contact with some people who had wheat straw for sale. Really it was too good for calves, but the owners wanted rid of it, and we therefore agreed a purchase at the right price.

The final batch that I ever reared for Mr. Capper came in at the beginning of December 1983.They did O.K. until the beginning to January 1984. Then I noticed that one calf would drink all its milk and then eat a little hay before it regurgitated. Dad came and looked at the calf and we felt a lump in its throat. I can still see Dad put some tongs down the calves throat and retrieve a complete ball of hay which had become lodged there, and it was this that was causing all the animals feeding problems.

Mr. Harris, who had always been Mr. Cappers calf dealer, knew of a chap called David Hughes who came from Docklow (which is between Bromyard and Leominster) and the latter wanted Fresian Bull calves reared, which would eventually be taken on for bull beef.

Mr. Hughes came over to check our facilities, and was happy to shake hands on an agreement for me to rear for him. The initial batch came in at the end of January, beginning of February. They were little trouble to get to drink, which is often the case with pure bred Fresians. They arrived in a couple of batches, and the unit was full within the week.

This type of calf grew rapidly, they were getting the usual milk morning and evening, and they were also started on Quicklets calf pellets, a handful to begin with which rapidly developed into ad lib feeding.

They were weaned at just over five weeks, and then went into the loose boxes. After cleaning out the pens ready to take more calves I contacted Roger Gough a neighbour about supplying calves, and he agreed to come down the following day and make the necessary arrangements. Three or four days went by, and although my parents and I called at his house to clarify the situation, he still didn't come down as promised.

In the meantime the stockman from Lower Hope Farm, Phil Prees rang up, wanting to know if we were in a position to rear more calves. Phil had previously been with Mr. Capper. As my neighbour kept on hovering about making a decision I agreed to rear for Phil Prees.

As happens, no sooner had we made the agreement with Phil Prees, than Roger Gough turned up with his representative, ready to make an arrangement, but I had to inform him that as he had kept hovering I had agreed to rear for another supplier.

Phil came over towards the end of April and brought some Hay, Straw, and Cake ready for his batch of calves. He then brought the calves over in two batches by Land Rover and trailer. They were quite small Hereford/Fresians calves and drank reasonably well.

Meanwhile, the Fresian bull calves loose in the boxes were continuing to shoot up on ad lib feed, and likewise the muck was growing. A couple of the bull calves one had to be quite wary of, as they could really chase you round, and give a good hard butt.

It was quite nice Spring weather, and a pleasure to be out and about feeding the calves. It gave one the incentive to get finished about six o clock, and depending on what time we had a meal, go for a walk with the dogs.

The pirate radio station "Radio Sunshine" that had been illegally broadcasting in our area for about a year, and proving very elusive to track down in such a rural area, as they were getting early warning signals from the locals, added a little excitement to the mundane tasks. I listened as I was going about my daily tasks, something different and local. The signal from the radio station proved to be so powerful that my brother Rupert, who lived in the south of England could also pick up the broadcasts. I found it all good fun, wondering if the would be caught.

When David Hughes', by now huge, calves left, I was pleased at how well they had done, but they left me a legacy of a mountain of muck. I know the saying goes that"Where there's muck there's Brass" but I've never seen any of it.

Dad came to my assistance with the tractor and fork, borrowed a trailer, and cleared the muck out of the buildings. The building was then left empty for about a week, and then fresh bedding was put down. Normally I had a couple of other boxes that I could use first, as I tried to rotate the loose boxes in use.

I would stop the next calves to be weaned milk for a few days, although they continued to get their Quicklet pellets. I found this method helped to calm them down, before I moved them to their new boxes.

Mr. Cappers Estate was in the hands of the land agents Strutt and Parker and I went to the sale one Friday afternoon at the beginning of July. I went the usual way on my two feet, and using my thumb!! I got a lift all the way to Hereford, and the sale was being held in the Green Dragon Hotel, Broad Street. The sale commenced, but as it did not reach the reserve price, was withdrawn. I subsequently heard that there were quite a few people still interested, but the sale was not finalised until early the following year.

A second batch of bull calves arrived from David Hughes towards the end of August, and the whole procedure began again.

The person who bought Mr. Cappers Estate was a Mr. Richardson, Managing Director of Harris Tractors, who were agents for Ford Tractors. Dad and I went to the Farm Implement Sale, towards the end of January 1985, we actually bumped into Mr. Lapper, who gave us two tickets for a free coffee each!! However, we didn't make any machinery purchases, but I enjoyed the event. The estate officially changed hands on the second February 1985.

However before the changeover - John Llewellyn, who was remaining as the Farm Manager on the estate, had arranged for me to rear 28 calves (a full unit) for Mr. Richardson - so I was pleased to be getting some continuity of work. Mr. Harris was still the calf dealer, but these calves were the smallest I had ever had from him, and price seemed to have dictated their purchase, but this made my job difficult, as this type of calf does not make for easy rearing. Some calves drink but others can be very difficult.

Towards the end of February, disaster happened. The pirate radio station "Radio Sunshine" was closed down !!!! Personally I think that is why we had a dull, cloudy summer that year !!!

So began a period of regularity of batches of calves. Alternately I had a batch of bull calves from David Hughes, followed by a batch for Mr. Richardson, and finally a batch from Lower Hope Farm. Then the sequence began all over again.

This proved to be a good steady period for me, and I really enjoyed my work. Having established regular batches, this gave me a break from chasing after work and wondering where the next batch was coming from. Having now built up a reputation for rearing good quality calves I had steady work, and with the new building, I now had an excellent working environment both for myself and the calves.

A further lean-to was added to the main building in which to store hay, straw, and also provide cover for the tractor. We made a good crop of hay. The person who lived at the Lodge, Alwyn Witby, came and turned the hay and kept shaking it out, until we eventually decided it was ready to bale. A couple of weeks after we had managed to clear off all the bales, Alwyn put a few of his sheep on our field, which kept it nicely cropped.

I had decided that although I should have liked to continue rearing a few of my own beef for the fatstock market, I just would not have the time or the space to justify this enterprise.

The calf rearing sequence I had developed took me throughout 1985, and into 1986, and then a bombshell. Father thought of putting the Coach House up for sale. He had seen a small farm in poor condition, about six miles out of Tenbury, that he thought we could build up. Heather was about to get hitched to her boyfriend Glyn, and they were looking for a place to start work on, and it was thought that maybe we could all go in together.

It just about broke my heart, as it had taken me years to build up steady contracts, and a good reputation, and having at last achieved a good set of buildings compatible with my working routine, it was all to be thrown away, to start again from scratch. Although I voiced my opinion, and though they were bloody mad, I just got on with the job in hand and shut up, hoping against hope that it would never happen.

Sadly David Hughes' wife died, and as a result he decided that he didn't want any more calves reared for a period, so that was a further blow to my world.

It was now the beginning of May 1986. Our small holding was put up for sale, and a buyer was found. However, by the time the architect had drawn up the plans for all that was required to be done to the new farm, which we called "Bache Farm" it was going to prove too expensive to be a worthwhile enterprise.

Meanwhile our small holding was reaching exchange of contracts stage, and Mum and Dad began a period of tearing around, uphill and down dale for miles, looking for new premises. I still kept my head down, thinking this was only a bad dream and couldn't possibly come to fruition. Dad was pressurising the would be purchasers of the Coach House to complete, as my parents thought that they had found a place.

I was horrified by it. The farm was miles from anywhere, in very wild state, and would need a tremendous amount of time money and effort put in to provide anything like the set up that I was currently with. Fortunately for me parents were gazzumped over this property, and so they had had to resort to further searches.

Heather and Glyn had by this time decided to set up on their own, which meant that a smaller property was now all that was required, and parents finally purchased a bungalow with land in Lucton which they thought would be suitable.

However all was not resolved as the buyer for the Coach House changed his mind and purchased another property. I thought thank goodness, there was now no good reason at all for us to move, but it was not to be.

Parents went ahead and bought the bungalow anyway. It was the end of October 1986 before I was taken across to view the bungalow, and we still owned the Coach House.

I still didn't think that the bungalow would serve all our needs, I felt it was very isolated compared with Rochford but I wasn't in a position to make a great protest, so I continued to just shut up, and get on with the day to day tasks at the Coach House. The calves needed my attention, and they gave me something to concentrate on while everything was happening around me.

Having purchased the bungalow, Dad was busily engaged trying to draw up plans, for the building of a calf unit This would entail the removal and levelling of a great deal of soil, to one side of the bungalow. However as the Coach House was still for sale, the months went by and it was actually February 1987 before a date was arranged to start work levelling the site.

I'm getting ahead of myself as it was late 1986 that Father bought and had installed an aga and we spent the next few months going to and fro between both properties. Still I hoped and prayed that it would all go away.

It was quite a severe winter again, and I recall frozen water on all the calf buckets, which necessitated, a kick with the boot to each bucket as I went on my rounds.

We had new neighbours as the Mount changed hands again. It was bought by Jill O'Brien and Mike Tyson (not the boxer!!). The former was a nurse at Tenbury hospital and had two children, a girl aged about thirteen called Clare and a boy about nine called Jonathan. Mike also had a son by a previous marriage called Nathan and he was about twelve at the time. I thought that they were really nice neighbours.

The children had a great time the day the school bus failed to turn up due to snowy conditions - a bonus days sledging.

I was finding it difficult to keep my footing as I fed the calves in the slippery conditions. The tread had worn off the underside of my wellington boots and this added to my problems. I got fed up of going base over apex onto my bum all the time, so I took a Thursday afternoon off, and went into Tenbury to Midland Shire Farmers and purchased a new pair of wellington boots. These were a great improvement, I was able to stand up and walk about without hitting the deck all the time.

As work commenced on levelling the site at the bungalow the rainy season started, and it rained and it rained. The contractors had a very difficult job to level the site as it was sloping, and they had to put down tons and tons of stones to prevent the base sinking.

April came and we thought that we had a couple to purchase the Coach House. They came from Bristol, and although they had a property to sell, they felt that the latter would sell straightaway. However, although they got a purchaser, we got involved in a chain, and after about six weeks, the would be purchasers of the Bristol property dropped out, so we were back to square one.

Fortunately I had continued to keep my head down and carry on as normal rearing calves regardless. Just as well really, because I would have gone 'BLOODY MAD with all the ifs and buts, and stops and starts.

On the strength of all that was going on I took in another batch of bull calves from David Hughes during the second week in May.

On Saturday June 13th Heather and Glyn "tied the knot" at Little Hereford Church, and the reception was at their Farm. The Special School had a barn which had been modernised, in order to provide the facilities for functions.The following day a Sunday we were all recovering, but Dad had to go and Judge a Working Hunter class at a local show, and on the Monday both parents went with a friend to the "Three Counties Show, Malvern - this proved to be a busy time.

Jim and Doreen our friends from Yorkshire had come over for the wedding and also stayed to attend the Three Counties Show. I attended the show on the Tuesday, and had a good look round, as always it was the cattle sections that I found held the most interest. It was a real pleasure to be at the show on a good day weatherwise. Some years the showground can be very muddy and trampled.

During the cattle judging I met Mr. Richardson the owner of Lower Hope Estate, and we had a chat, but as usual I couldn't stay late as there were always calves waiting to be fed. Typically when I turned my back for a day, two of the calves had pushed out the restraining bar at the front of the pen, and had got out, but fortunately no further than the passage.

The next day David Hughes came to collect this batch of calves, and both of us were pleased at how well they had done.

This meant that I now had empty pens all calves having left the premises.

Another buyer emerged for the Coach House. These people had already sold their property, and had been looking round for some time. The lady was keen to keep horses, and liked the look of our loose boxes, and she and her husband decided to purchase, so our proposed move became reality.

Now we really embarked on mamouth task. Firstly the pens had to be mucked out, and then dismantled. The plan being to take down the calf building at the Coach House block by block and then re-erect it at Lucton on the prepared base.

My parents moved out of the Coach House on Monday June 22nd 1987. However, most of the calf buildings still had to be dismantled, so this meant Dad and I going to and fro, bringing across parts of the building, ready to reassemble.

Andrew Allen who had done some contract baling and hedge-cutting for us in the past also helped and we utilised his tractor and trailer to cart across concrete blocks to Lucton.

The steel work was dismantled by a contractor at the Coach house and re-erected at Lucton, and then it was a question of re-levelling and moving more stone to get a good base.

We altered the original design a little, where we had previously had all blockwork, we now put down only two rows of blockwork with timber on the top, to form the sides.

We also added a further building to the site to house the tractor, loose calves and straw, thereby dispensing with the lean-to buildings we had at the Coach House.

After about three weeks we virtually had the buildings up, but the floor still needed concreting. However, before this could be done we received an invitation to have a holiday from Harry and Shirley in Yorkshire (Mum and Dad taught them to ride when they were running the riding school in West Kirby). I hadn't had a holiday for years and years, I quite enjoyed the break. Then it was back to reality and completing the calf buildings.

Dad thought that the timber partitions for the calf pens having been left out and exposed to the weather for the best part of three months, would have been cleaned off, no such luck. I spent a great deal of time scraping off and hosing down before the partitions were clean enough to put into the building.

Unfortunately I would have to resort to mixing up the milk powder in the kitchen of the bungalow, as there was no water laid on to the calf buildings. This meant invading the kitchen twice a day and man handling all the buckets to the pens. This was particularly hard on Mum, as although she didn't complain, she was not feeling well, and its impossible not to spill some water and powder as you mix up and carry buckets. Fortunately I had by now an electric mixer for the powder so that was an improvement.

We were virtually ready for me to take my first batch of calves at Lucton at about the beginning of October. David Hughes sent over a number of batches of bull calves over a period of a week until we had thirty in number, so things were getting underway again.

As well as getting the calves established on their feeding routines we also had to set about concreting the floor of the second building which would eventually house the loose calves. Fortunately, this time we resorted to Ready Mix. The concrete arriving at intervals, so Dad, myself and a friend Edward Jackson set about levelling and tamping down the loads.

We also set in a septic tank to take the effluent from the calves, and as Dad is a perfectionist, it all took some time. It was actually a very exhausting time for me, because over a six week period as well as doing all the jobs connected with the building, I still had my calf feeding routine. There was still milk powder to be mixed, and carried round twice a day. I was also working in darkness at both ends of the day.

Mum still wasn't feeling well. She went to see the doctor, and he advised a spell of bed rest. However around Christmas when she still wasn't improving, she saw a second Doctor, and he sent her to the hospital for tests and Xrays. In the early part of January 1988, she went for further tests. This time to East Birmingham Hospital and sadly this is when Cancer was diagnosed. Meanwhile, Mum was still determined to help if she could, and we moved the first batch of weaned calves over to the new loose boxes with Mums help.

This meant that I was now ready to take in the next batch of calves as soon as I had done all the usual mucking out. This is when I realised how much harder the mucking out was going to be than at Rochford, where the logistics of the building and the fall of the ground had aided the mucking out process. At Lucton I found that it was taking three times as long because all the manure had to be forked out, and lifted upwards into the trailer, and then carted to the muck heap in the field. In fairness I had actually realised all this before the buildings were erected, but had been over ruled, and now my feelings were vindicated.

Roy Rogers came and steam cleaned the calf house, after I had removed the manure. I had found that this was the most effective way between calf batches, and the former always did a good tidy job. In came the second batch of bull calves again supplied by a dealer called Mr. Rudge on behalf of David Hughes, so this meant that just before Christmas 1987 I was full of calves in both buildings.

Due to Mums illness, we entered 1988 all feeling very sombre. Dad was going to and fro to the hospital in Birmingham taking Mum for her tests, and towards the end of February she had to spend a week in the hospital.

I continued to be kept very busy with all the calf pens full. The family came over to visit when they could, all naturally very concerned about Mums illness.

I also found that I missed Rochford area for my walks. I could walk around our field at Lucton which took about five minutes. I found that the roads were too narrow for pleasurable walking. At that time we had a whippet called Spinney, and if she dashed off into a field and then returned to the road, it could be dangerous on the narrow bends, so I just started going round and round the field.

The first lot of calves left the farm. They were collected by David Hughes, and he was very pleased with the result. This meant that after cleaning out the loose pens the weaned calves could be moved on.

It was about this time that mum started her Chemotherapy at Cheltenham Hospital. She had to be taken three times a week by father for the treatment. I didn't drive and had always relied on others for transport, and I began to feel really caged in. However I couldn't say how I felt as Mum was so very ill.

Eventually after about a month, towards the end of March, Dad took me into Hereford to the market, and I realised how much I had missed being able to go there, and it really helped to meet up with old acquaintances, and blew a lot of cobwebs away for an hour or two.

Just before Mums birthday on the 17th April she was in terrible pain during the night, and she had to be rushed to Hereford County hospital, she remained in Hereford for a week and then Dad took Mum to Cheltenham again for a further session of Chemotherapy. This seemed to ease the pain temporarily.

The next event on the calendar that year was Kingsland Show. Dad was on the committee and it was held on a field owned by Mr. Coates. This field had been an orchard, and before it could be used safely for horse events, a great deal of timber and small branches had to be removed. Dad volunteered our services and muggins got lumbered with cleaning up the ground. We also made a water trough for the event. Dad and I dug out the ground, mixed the concrete with the aid of a cement mixer, and to the best of my knowledge, it still holds water today!!

The show was held on the Saturday before the bank holiday towards the end of May. The weather was quite warm, I had fed all my calves and could have gone with my parents, but decided I had seen enough of the showground, and so I stayed at home and shovelled mu.........ck.

That year we didn't require any hay, as I had settled down to a pattern of rearing solely for David Hughes bull calves, and as a result we no longer needed bales of hay.

The Three Counties Show was one of the few away days for me that year. Although I would have liked to continue to go to Hereford and Kidderminster markets, it proved to be too difficult. The main road past Lucton was quite a fast road, with no suitable verges to stand on and hail a lift. I found that I could be standing for ages waiting, and also I wasn't on a very direct route for either market.

June came and went and Dad took his horse jumps, that he had made to a number of small shows for the horse and pony jumping events. Mum accompanied him if she could, now that Dad had retired he was going to more shows, and that year we all went to the Royal Show. I was able to go to the latter, as now that I was only getting batches from one source, if there was no follow up batch, I could be out of calves completely from time to time, and this proved to be the case this year. It was many years since I had last been free to go to the "Royal" and I thoroughly enjoyed my day.

The following week I went to visit my old school at Exhall Grange, Coventry, just to say "Hello" to the staff. This meant that Dad took me to Leominster to catch a bus to Birmingham. The trip took two and a half hours as it went via Ludlow, Cleobury Mortimer, etc. etc. I caught a train to Coventry from Birmingham, and finally another bus from Coventry city centre to Exhall Grange. My visit was very brief, as I then had to trail all the way back home again, but it was good to see people again if only for a very short time. This trip proved to me how difficult it was for me to get anywhere from Lucton.

Father bought a Peugeot 205 diesel van which only had two seats, and so if there were three of us travelling I had to sit in the back, but I found that I couldn't stick it for long as it made me feel so sick. This again added to my feeling of being caged in and isolated.

However, at the end of July my parents and I went north to Appleby in Westmorland, for a few days, which made a nice break. Fortunately, my sister Heather loaned us her Volkswagon Golf for the trip or I wouldn't have gone.

We had such a good time that Mum said that she thought we should have a repeat visit again soon. On our return journey, Mum was not feeling well for the last few miles, so as soon as we arrived home she went to bed. The next day she got up, and went to do a little shopping, but still felt unwell, and was in a lot of pain. The doctor was called, and he had her admitted to hospital in Hereford.

The following Saturday, it was the beginning of August and the

Tenbury Wells Show was scheduled. I went to the show, and on returning home it hit me, how very lonely the bungalow felt without Mum. She was in hospital for three and a half weeks. Dad visited her once or twice every day. I went almost every day, until one evening on Dad and my return from the hospital, I saw some straw sticking out of one of the calf house doors. I realised that some calves had been delivered in our absence. This meant that I was back in business with the calves, but made it more complicated to visit mum.

Mr.Rudge the calf dealer for David Hughes completed delivering the calves over about ten days and then we had our full intake.

Mum's legs were very swollen and painful, and her surgeon said that he didn't think that the family would be able to cope, if she returned home, but we brought her home anyway, which was her wish, and we were given morphine for her pain control.

Mum went to a few more shows with Dad, but was unable to get out of the car at these events. Dad went to judge at the Peterborough Show, but Mum was not able to go as she was continuing to deteriorate. It was about a week after Dad's return that Mum died at 1-45 p.m. on the 14th September. Even though we knew how ill she was, it was still a terrible shock. Dad had just been dozing in the other room, and when he went into the bedroom Mum had gone.

The funeral was a week later, at Hereford Crematorium. The family, and quite a few friends, neighbours, and people that mum had known through her time with the pony club attended. The family and a very few close friends returned to the bungalow. A number of people had travelled long distances to attend. Mum, had reached 64 years old the previous April, so it was a further tragedy to lose her at a relatively young age. Even after the funeral I had to feed the calves as they could not be ignored.

Dad and I now had to try and pick Up our lives, and learn to cope without mum. Dad took over the cooking, even though I had often done some cooking with mum. Rice pudding was my speciality, however I didn't argue, and anyway I had my calves to look after.

Dads cooking had its ups and downs. He actually was quite a good cook, but had a tendency to put the chicken carcass into the aga to make soup, and also soften the bones which he would then liquidise for the dogs. The trouble was that he often forgot it was in the aga, and the result was a dry blackened charcoal dish, and this was repeated time and time again.

I moved the calves from the pens into the loose boxes, and Dad went to stay with friends for a few days, so I had to look after myself the dogs and the calves, but there was plenty to do, which helped me through this period. I was able to go over to my eldest sister Elizabeth's for the odd meal, and Heather also kept in touch with me, as she was living in Orleton at the time.

Yet again I cleaned out the calf pens, ready to receive another batch of calves. Roy Rogers, came along and completed the job with his steam cleaner.

Mr. Rudge the calf dealer brought over some calves virtually as soon as the pens were dried out and ready. At the same time David Hughes purchased calves at Gloucester market, so the pens were full in just under a week this time, which is the way I preferred things. Ideally, I liked all the calves delivered together, as although I was very busy it made for better calf management overall. However, on the plus side Mr. Rudge knew exactly the type of calf David Hughes required, and this is why sometimes it was only possible to get three or four together.

As usual it took only a few days to get all the calves drinking from the bucket. The fresian calves are much quicker at getting the idea, especially if I used a dummy teat. The Hereford cross are more docile calves, but much more difficult to get drinking.

Dad started feeding the loose calves, and this enabled me to get on with the young calves in the pens uninterrupted.

Dad helping was a mixed blessing, he wouldn't go into the bull calf loose boxes as I did, he simply stood on a bale, cut the string of another bale, and threw it over the top of the rail. What a pantomime, the calves would be jumping around onto each other in an effort to snatch at the straw.

Checking the calves one evening, as I always did last thing. I found a heap of straw where Dad had thrown it with the calves lying on top of it, whilst by the manger it was all mucky - this was Dad's fault for just throwing it into one pile and not spreading it out as I would have done - not to worry it wasn't a matter of life or death, but it was very irritating.

This batch of calves went through without a problem, and so it was just before Christmas that I filled up with calves again, which meant that once again I was busy over the festive season.

Dad and I had planned to go to the Compasses Pub in Wigmore that year, but Heather and Glyn invited us to join them at Orleton for Christmas dinner.

1989 dawned and I saw the New Year in from my bed !!! I had my ups and downs with the batch of calves in at that time, but struggled on. Likewise it was very hard for Dad trying to come to terms with having lost Mum, in fact we both realised how much she had done for us. She had always helped me with the weaning of the calves, and also giving their injections when necessary.

Most Wednesdays Dad and I started going regularly to Hereford. Dad did the shopping and I went round the market this enabled me to keep up with the prices and meet acquaintances.

It proved to be not a bad winter, only a little snow fell, and temperatures generally were not too cold, so I didn't experience too much trouble with iced up buckets etc.

During that winter Dad and I occasionally went over to John Coates field at Kingsland, where the horse show was held, and cleared further branches and trees that had blown down. We logged up the wood and brought it back to use on the sitting room fire. This was not very successful at times, as the wood being apple would spit, and sparks jumped out of the fire. I really missed the efficiency of the wood burning stove that we had at the Coach house in Rochfort.

Spring came, and as well as looking after the calves we continued to go over to Kingsland to clear the field for the Show which was due to be held in May.

I was still churning out bull calves provided by David Hughes. These were normally Fresians but occasionally he put in a Charolais, Limosin, or Belgian blue (just to pep up the calf house with a different colour!!)

Dad and I were beginning to establish a routine. We did have a lady to clean when Mum was ill, and she returned to us for a little while but then left to concentrate on her main job which was re upholstering furniture so we continued on our own. We had by now got a dishwasher, so that made life easier.

During the Spring Dad continued to make up his jumps, these were made from poles and brushwood, and were very much in demand at local horse shows, where he also acted as a judge. He usually made fresh jumps every year, selling the old ones in the autumn sometimes to the show organisers and sometimes to private buyers.

In July Rupert my brother arranged a holiday weekend for the two of us in Holland. I travelled by local bus from Hereford to Gloucester, changed to a coach to London, where I was met by my brother. I stayed overnight at his home, and the following day he drove us in his car to Harwich, where we boarded an evening ferry to the hook of Holland.

This was my first trip abroad, and I found Holland very flat, but it was very enjoyable to get a chance to do something different. I was able to get away from home at that time because all the calves had been weaned, so it was only the loose calves that needed feeding and Dad was able to undertake that task.

It was a very hot summer that year, and its just as well Holland was flat because we did a great deal of walking around. I greatly appreciated my brother arranging the trip - and I had a break, however short from looking after calves.

I had an uneventful trip home, and found that Dad had not had any major problems with the calves. A few days later that batch of calves left the premises, so it was then back to the old routine, of cleaning out before we were ready to take another batch. However during the intervening time Dad and I fitted in a few days holiday in Appleby, and I always enjoyed so much meeting up with old friends and neighbours.

The end of August saw the intake of a new batch of calves. I now only took in four batches of Bull calves a year, which gave me brief breaks from rearing, but reduced my income.

In that batch I only had one serious problem. Checking the calves one Saturday evening, I noticed a calf had blown, so I tubed it twice to no avail. I then called out the vet Mr. Horlock, from Leominster. He came and de-gassed the calf. We thought all was well, I gave the calf a small drench, the vet left. Half an hour later I checked the calf, only to find that it had died.

Over the years I had occasional problems like this, once it was a calf with a twisted gut, and once it was caused by the feeding pellets.

I carried on with the calves throughout the autumn, and Dad and I decided to have our Christmas Dinner at home that year.

Dad cooked the turkey with all the trimmings. We put on paper hats, and drank red wine. In the afternoon I had a good dose, and then it was back to reality, and calf feeding time again.

It was during that year that my brother and father thought that we should sell the bungalow and calf unit, because of finances.

However, I had more than enough of moving and decisions made over my head, and so I dug my heels in against any further moves. My eldest sister Elizabeth saw how very upset I was, and as a result, both sisters supported me in my resistance to further disruption. So, although the bungalow went onto the market briefly, it was then withdrawn.

Moving on to the New Year and 1990 - the start of a new decade. We ticked over for about four months, going over to John Coates field, collecting wood, and father continuing to make fresh horse jumps, while I continued to rear my bull calves.

The batch in at that time only consisted of 20 calves, as the dealer buying on behalf of David Hughes couldn't get sufficient suitable calves at the same time, so I was not fully employed, and economically the return would be considerably reduced.

Unfortunately for me, as I had time on my hands, Dad found gardening, and lawn mowing jobs for me, which I hated !!!

The Spring progressed and I think it was on the 20th May, anyway it was a Monday, that dad went into Leominster, and, while he was away, we had a delivery of Calf cake. The latter arrived on a lorry in 25 kilo bags, and I went to assist the driver unload. I stood on the back of the lorry on a pallet, lifting up the sacks and then throwing them to the driver, who was stacking them into a container in our yard. All of a sudden I caught my foot in the pallet, and toppled down onto the ground off the lorry, hitting my head and causing a large gash to my head.

The lorry driver rushed in and phoned the emergency services for an ambulance, and I was taken to the Hereford General Hospital Casualty department where I received 19 stitches.

Meanwhile Father returned only to find the bungalow unlocked and me missing. He went around calling my name, and our neighbour Harold came round and explained that I had had an accident and been taken to hospital.

I had weighed out the milk powder ready for the calves evening feed, and already put it in the mixer, however, rumour has it that Dad and Harold, having no idea of the correct ratio of water to powder, mixed up a ration with more luck than good judgement. (anyway the calves didn't show any adverse effects !!). Father then rushed into the Hospital to see how I was faring.

A young doctor stitched me up, but I remember that it was a very kind nurse called Adele Griffiths, who talked to me and helped ease the trauma.

I also became friendly with a lady secretary who came up to the ward to which I was admitted (the ward was called Victoria Ward) and her role was to take details of my accident. I still occasionally pop in for a chat when I am in Hereford with a few minutes to spare, as I like to retain links with a number of nurses that I met previously when I was in Harry Davies Ward for my knee operation.

I remained in hospital for two days observation before returning home on a Wednesday afternoon. At home father fed the calves for the first day, and then because he was busy with a commitment to Kingsland show, I had to get on and feed the calves on my own, and anyway I didn't like sitting about especially when I knew there was work that just had to be done.

The district nurse came the following Tuesday, after the Monday Bank Holiday to remove my stitches - it wasn't painful - You know what they say, "No sense, no feeling, no feeling, no sense."

I made a good recovery, and we weaned the calves, which fortunately showed no effects from their feeding hiccup !!

Once again we went to the Three Counties Show, Dad taking his jumps for the Working Hunters, and I spent my time around the cattle exhibits. Jim and Doreen, our friends from Yorkshire were again staying with us for the duration of the show. The men went for all three days of the show, but Doreen and I found one day sufficient.

July came, and as father had another commitment at a show. I attended the wedding of a girl cousin in the south of England, travelling down with my sister Heather and her husband. It was only a small wedding but I enjoyed the occasion.

Later on in July, Dad and I went up North for a few days, to see friends, while I was once again between batches of calves.

August arrived, and as usual Tenbury Show is always held on the first Saturday in August, its always part of my itinerary to attend - Tenbury Show wouldn't be the same without me, I've been going so long, that I now get free admission - "I GO WITH THE SHOW" Father dropped me off at the showground, and the arrangement was that I would make my own way back. The pure bred Hereford Cattle are always a particularly good class at Tenbury, especially commendable as it is a relatively small one day agricultural show. I enjoy making my selection of potential prizewinning cattle entries, and seeing if the judges agree with me.

The following week I could be found once again preparing pens to take in another batch of bull calves. They again came in dribs and drabs as there were still a shortage of good quality bull calves about, eventually we had our quota of twenty or thereabouts.

We had also established a vegetable patch. Dad did all the rotovating and planting, whereas I poor devil was expected to do all the picking!! Surplus peas and beans all went into the freezer. Initially we blanched the vegetables, but eventually just topped and tailed the beans, then put them through the slicer and into the freezer.

Spinney, my sister Heathers whippet (that I looked after), and Mackie our next door farming neighbours cairn terrier, used to amuse me at this time of the year. They went off daily from about 7-30 a.m. to 3-30 p.m. when they reappeared exhausted, after a day spent chasing rabbits, they repeated this practice daily at this time of the year. Mackie then disappeared for a few weeks worn out by all his activities, only to reappear and whisper to me that a pair of stilts would be useful for Christmas, as he had a very hard time keeping up with the whippet on such short legs so I passed this information onto his owners Harold and Carol !!!

I also attended Tenbury Christmas Fatstock Show, I am always fascinated watching the judges pick out the winning beasts, and again I try to pick out the winners myself, and sometimes the judges agree with me.

It was during the winter of 1990 just prior to Christmas that I had a batch of calves in, and during this time we had heavy snow and the electricity went off during one night, and didn't come on again until daylight, which was well after eight o clock. Meanwhile I had all the calves to feed in the dark, and all the powder to mix by hand - so they didn't have a very strong mix that day as it was too difficult to mix up all the powder to the correct strength by hand.

The new year entered on a very cold note, and unfortunately we had some virus pneumonia in the loose calves. The cold weather upsets them and their steamy breath causes the infection to spread. We lost one calf as a result, and it set the others back, however they did all leave at the twelve week target.

This brought us to the end of January, and then it was back to the usual mucking out routine, but on this occasion everything was hampered by the weather, from mucking out the loose pens to the freezing up of the water buckets in the individual pens.

When the weather was like this I had found from experience to just give the calves a little water, and tip away any not drunk, a short while later, but, I couldn't persuade Dad to cooperate on this - his idea was to give the calves warm water, but this could cause the calves to drink too quickly, and so cause more problems than it solved.

We struggled on with the calves throughout this cold spell

putting lots of straw under the calves and fitting lids made of plywood over the tops of the pens, which were held down by bales of straw, thus preventing the calves from dislodging the timber lids. This method succeeded in keeping the calves much warmer and cosier in their pens.

Unfortunately I had to get the vet out to this batch, as some of them became reluctant to drink and were running high temperatures. A few calves had to have a glucose solution piped down their throats as they wouldn't drink, this was very time consuming, we battled on for a few days which sometimes felt like forever, however eventually all the calves recovered, and then you quickly forget all the worries of the past few days. Dad helped me throughout this period as well as doing all the cooking and any essential household tasks.

Time ticked by and the calves grew, and became too big for the individual pens, so we weaned them, and then they were moved on to the larger loose pen. Initially they always charge about enjoying the increased space and freedom before they settle down.

As soon as the individual pens were free I repeated the mucking out routine. Dad helped me on this occasion, and we forked the manure straight into the muck spreader, which had been left in the yard by our neighbour Harold, and when it was full the latter drove it away and spread it on his own fields.

As the weather improved and Spring approached Father started making his jumps again, and the year progressed on a similar pattern to the previous year.

We attended the usual shows, and Hereford market on regular basis.

In the heat of the summer, during the month of August, Dad attended the Burwarton Show on the first Thursday, and I went along to help, as I was between batches of calves. Dad went to judge out in the open field, and he was standing out in the full sun from about 1 p.m. to 5 p.m without a drink being taken to him. At the end of the competition, we loaded up the drinks and returned home, where Dad immediately drank a great deal of fluid in a rush, and then felt very faint and sick, obviously suffering from sun stroke.

He rang the doctor, who gave him some pills, and told him to stay in bed, and as a result he had to cancel taking his jumps to the Angelsey Show. Meanwhile I looked after myself foodwise, Dad didn't feel like eating, but I made sure that he had plenty to drink, and after a few days he recovered.

September came and Jim and Doreen our friends from Yorkshire came to stay. During their stay Dad realised that he was running out of pills and he would have to go to the Doctor to get a repeat prescription. While he was away Jim and I realised that the red pills he was swallowing looked like Smarties so we counted how many were left and replaced them with red smarties. The next morning we were having our breakfast, and we watched Dad get his pills ready to swallow them, I had to look away for laughing as I saw Dad take a swig of water and swallow his Smartie pill completely oblivious of the change. Kim burst out laughing, and eventually we confessed, but Dad wouldn't believe that they were Smarties - so Jim showed him his real tablets.

The night before Jim and Doreen returned home, I received the first few of the next batch of calves. David Hughes also brought some of the new big bales, which were a bit more difficult for me to handle on my own, in a small area, but it was good straw.

Jim and Doreen being early birds set off between 4 and 4-30a.m. the next morning and as I could already hear the new calves bawling, I got up, made a cup of tea and started on teaching the new calves to drink from a bucket, sometimes a lengthy process for the first day or so.

I successfully reared these calves without too many problems, and then we had a further batch in at the beginning of

November. I was able that year to move the calves into the loose pen just before Christmas which made life easier. Just before Christmas Dad was driving back from meeting some of his pals when he had a dizzy spell and nearly blacked out, just avoiding an accident.

As a result he went to the doctor, and the doctor ceased his pills as apparently they could cause this sort of side effect.

Once again we catered for ourselves over the Christmas period, and we made sure that we had lots to eat and also had a good rest in front of the television.

The Thursday after New Year (which incidently I saw in at home with Dad and we just had a drink to toast the occasion before retiring) Dad went to collect the post and handed me a letter from Littlewoods Pools, and surprise, surprise I had won £400 - What a nice new year present. I refrained from going out and having a mad spending spree - I simply put it in the hands of the "Black Horse Bank" for a rainy day.

I carried on mucking out the calves as per usual, and this was followed by a visit from Roy Rogers and his steam cleaner - the latter always gave a nice clean fresh atmosphere on completion, and this greatly reduced the risk of infection in the next batch.

It was during the early part of the year that we had a great deal of heavy rain and as the ground was still fairly hard after the drought of the previous year, the rain ran off the top rather than soaking in, as a result our pond overflowed and the lane became flooded to a depth of 18".

More calves arrived and they settled in and were doing alright, and we were satisfactorily progressing through February when Dad returned from Bromyard on a Thursday feeling unwell, so he decided to go to the surgery to see Doctor Matthias - the latter took his blood pressure, which revealed that there was a problem and had Dad admitted to the Hereford County Hospital for tests.

Dad remained in Hospital for two weeks, so I was now on my own coping with everything. My sisters came over when they could in order to take me to visit Dad. David Hughes the provider of our batches of calves also was good enough to visit Dad in hospital during this time.

However during this period I also began to feel unwell myself, so Harold our neighbour and his wife and children came over and helped me move the weaned calves into the big loose pen, which was just as well because I went down with a severe case of flu, and also had bad nose bleeds. The doctor came and told me to stay in bed, which I did as much as I could. Fortunately Harold was able to keep an eye on things and feed the calves in the loose pen.

Father returned home needing to take medication daily to help stabilise his condition. Meanwhile I staggered on doing my jobs, but not feeling really well for some time.

March arrived and David Hughes came to collect his batch of reared calves, and informed us that he would not be putting in any more batches, as he had recently bought some additional land which was adjacent to his property, and therefore did not have the capital for the time being to invest in the purchase of more calves.

This was a considerable blow to me, as David Hughes had been a good person to rear for, always providing me with a good basic bull calf to rear on.

However towards the end of April, as Dad was still recovering and I was out of calves, the former suggested that we went up, to Westmorland and Yorkshire to visit friends and have a break from our problems.

We had only returned home a short while, when we had the bad news that our neighbour from Westmorland days Bert Lewis had died, we were greatly saddened, but also so pleased that we had been able to call when we were in Westmorland to cheer him up.

It was the beginning of June when Harold our next door neighbour in Lucton, bought a small Charolais bull calf which he asked me to rear. I agreed and this was followed by twenty two more bull calves in dribs and drabs. This can some times be a tedious way for a batch of calves to arrive, but at least its not an all or nothing situation, when they come in like this.

I reared a further batch for Harold that year without any major problems and considered myself fortunate to have these batches as the calf market was generally depressed, and there wasn't much scope in the market for profit making.

Jim and Doreen visited again in September and as usual it was good to see them.

We progressed into 1993, unfortunately Dad had to go into hospital again during the early part of the year, and it was about that time that I finally became completely exasperated with the small open fire that we had in the sitting room. It was really designed to only take coal, but father would put on small logs which kept sparking and falling out - I really missed the wood burning stove that we had installed in the Coach House at Rochford, and decided that it was time to have a similar fire in the bungalow at Lucton.

A cousin of David Hughes worked for West Midland Farmers, and as they were able to quote a competitive price for a wood burning stove I decided to purchase one myself after consulting Dad.

We went to collect the fire from Hereford by car. Edward Jackson the builder who had put up the blockwork for our loose calf house, fitted the fire in during April, and I was more than pleased with the result. In fact Dad was also heard to comment, "Why, didn't we have one before."

Harold put in a further two batches during 1993, again he would purchase calves over a period of about two to three weeks. I didn't like getting the calves this way, but at least it was calves coming in to be reared.

I found the type of calf that I was now being asked to rear was considerably smaller than those put in by David Hughes in the past. The former were more difficult to rear on the whole. I found they could be more reluctant to start off drinking, and very often had a great deal more niggling problems.

Dad was obviously feeling lonely, after losing Mum five years previously, and during this period he had a lady friend, and she was followed by another lady friend called Mary, who obviously missed him so much when he had a further spell in hospital for a hernia operation, that there was talk of them getting hitched. The lady in question was actually eighteen months younger than myself, she had four children ranging in age between thirteen and twenty - two, and I liked her very much, she had a very nice personality, with a lot of wit, and she was also a good cook. !!!

We were only ticking over really after losing David Hughes calf rearing contract, and not really showing any profit for all the effort involved, and as calf prices were so poor, it was finally decided to put the bungalow and buildings onto the property market, at the beginning of December 1993.

My last batch of calves finally went through, and it was with very mixed feelings that I watched the lorry leave with my final batch on board, but the economics combined with everything else, made the decision necessary.

I kept myself occupied during this period the end of 1993 and the beginning of 94, doing jobs around the property ie. splitting wood, and general tidying up, Dad and I continued to go into Hereford once a week, and I always visited the market etc.

Life was indeed much less hectic, but I missed the routine, and personal satisfaction of seeing a well reared batch of calves leave the premises.

During this time I knew that I had a great many decisions to make - on the working front the calf rearing enterprise had been terminated so that was one aspect of my life resolved.

On the more personal level Dad and Mary had decided to get married and live in Stourbridge, Worcestershire - they did ask me to live with them, but it was a town environment, not far from the railway station. I had been born and reared in the countryside, and all my interests are centred on rural life - in fact I had found it very hard during my school years in Coventry to be in an urban area.

After the bungalow was sold I would in fact be homeless. I hoped to be able to take advantage of a bungalow specially adapted for a disabled person in Rochford, near Tenbury Wells. I would have really liked to have moved back to that area, as I had friends, and happy memories of my time in that location. However, due to Council policy my request was turned down.

I was now on the Council Housing list. Father and I thought that we had a purchaser for the bungalow who then unfortunately dropped out due to domestic differences. The bungalow then went up for sale by auction, but wasn't sold so at least I had a roof over my head for a bit longer.

Eventually, Leominster Marches Housing Association offered me a bungalow which had become available in Brimfield. I went out to visit the bungalow at the beginning of July 94, decided to accept, as I felt that I would be able to cope by myself and three weeks later moved in, bringing Spinney the whippet with me.

It was a big change - initially I very much missed company having always lived with the family or others during my school boarding days. However I decided that there was to be a new stage to my life so I must set about building up a new way of living.

Through contacts of my elder sister, I was introduced to "Lifestyle" and I expressed a wish to write my autobiography - feeling that now I had more time to reflect on the things that have occurred in my life to date. Often I felt that I should have like to have partaken more in decisions which so greatly affected my lifestyle, even though I have always been so grateful for the support of my family since my accident.

I have wondered on many occasions what life would have held for me had I not had my accident, but one has to put those feelings aside and get on with the day to day, and that is what I now actively intend to do.

I have joined a cookery class, attend on a regular basis adult Literacy class, ie. "Second Chance," made friends with local farmers, who I am always welcome to visit, and I try to help in small ways, answering the phone, taking deliveries if no one else is about. I still get to Hereford on a regular basis to keep my eye on the Livestock Market and hopefully keep up with acquaintances from times past. I also manage to get away on occasion to visit friends in the north of England which is always a great pleasure, and so as my final act before starting my new lifestyle I gave Father "Away" on the occasion of his marriage to start his new lifestyle.

Tim Montgomery,
October 1996.